Beate C. Kirchne

AF283977

111 Places
in Rio de Janeiro
That You Must
Not Miss

Photographs by Jorge Vasconcellos

111

© Emons Verlag GmbH
All rights reserved
All photos © Jorge Vasconcellos, exept:
Museu de Astronomia e Ciências Afins | MAST: ch. 76;
Tay Nacimento: ch. 21, ch. 29, ch. 81, ch. 91, ch. 96;
Alexandre Macieira: ch. 15, ch. 18, ch. 50, ch. 72,
ch. 80, ch. 87, ch. 89, ch. 95, ch. 99, ch. 104, ch. 107;
Alexandre Macieira | Riotur: ch. 39;
Beate C. Kirchner: ch. 1, ch. 3, ch 11, ch. 12, ch. 14, ch. 17,
ch. 19, ch. 20, ch. 22, ch. 25, ch. 26, ch. 28, ch. 32, ch. 34, ch. 38,
ch 40, ch. 41, ch. 46, ch 49, ch 51, ch 56, ch. 60, ch. 61,
ch. 64, ch. 65, ch. 85, ch. 94, ch. 102, ch. 103, ch. 109;
Ivo Korytowski: ch. 67, ch. 79, ch. 83, ch. 97;
Sonia Mibielli: ch. 52; Silvana Marques: ch. 78;
Depositphotos.com, mikelane45: ch. 86, Louis Perrin: ch. 6
© Cover motif: cobaltstock/Depositphotos.com
Edited by Karen E. Seiger
Printing und binding: Lensing Druck GmbH & Co. KG,
Feldbachacker 16, 44149 Dortmund
Design: Eva Kraskes, based on a design
by Lübbeke | Naumann | Thoben
Maps: altancicek.design, www.altancicek.de
Printed in Germany 2018
ISBN 978-3-7408-0262-2

Did you enjoy it? Do you want more?
Join us in uncovering new places around the world on:
www.111places.com

Foreword

Rio is called *Cidade Maravilhosa* – the marvelous city, embracing Guanabara Bay and Sugarloaf Mountain. The *joia de viver*, the wonderful spirit of the Cariocas, as Rio's residents are affectionately called, is contagious, and their enthusiasm for *futebol* legendary. Most visitors will already know about the giant statue of Christ the Redeemer, Copacabana Beach, and *Carnaval* before they arrive.

But who knows where the Cariocas meet downtown to dance at lunchtime? And where "maritime chicken" is served near the harbor? Where a *cachaça* sommelier chooses the range of nightcaps? Under which bridge in the northern outskirts the party is always jumping to a local version of R&B? And where the unofficial patron of the city, Saint George, is cheered on by 100,000 fans?

This guidebook will take you to 111 authentic places that Cariocas love.

But it will also take you to curious places that may surprise even the locals. To the bird cemetery on Paquetá Island, where pets from all over Brazil find their final resting place. To an enormous cathedral, where the pastor lands on the roof in a helicopter. Only very few people know where you can still find the Brazilian forerunner of *Playboy* magazine, and where believers go behind the altar to pray.

This book also invites you to meet some of the city's most extraordinary people. Expressionist painter Paulo Dallier will lead you through his enchanting neighborhood of Morro da Conceição; the grand master of baroque music Roberto de Regina performs private concerts in Barra de Guaratiba; and DJ Zezinho from the Rocinha *favela*, or slum, teaches loops and samples to local residents for free.

Go find the hidden places in *Rio Antigo*, Old Rio, the avant-garde art places, the pivotal sites in the eventful history of the city, as well as graffiti art that tell the stories of the *favelas*, and the best views of Guanabara Bay – all and more in this truly marvelous city.

111 Places

1__A Cena Muda Kiosk

Curious treasure trove

Adda Di Guimarães calls her kiosk A Cena Muda (A Change of Scene) partly in homage to the cinema magazine published from the 1920s through 1955, but also because it was a change of scene for Adda herself. She had run an antiques shop featuring autographed books and magazines in Ipanema until the rent finally became unaffordable. She decided without further ado to open the Banca de Revistas Antigas, or Antiquarian Magazines Kiosk, in 2003. After much bureaucratic confusion – old magazines aren't, according to the regulations, goods that can be sold at a kiosk – the mayor approved an exemption. He liked the idea.

The concept clicked and is one of a kind in Brazil today. Adda's antiques shop was already a port of call for a specialist audience, and they continued to shop at her kiosk, where theater lovers and cinema fanatics in particular are bound to find something of interest to them. Alongside culture and theater magazines, there are collectible picture cards from all eras, an impressive collection of Barbie Dolls, and a vinyl collection with some very rare disks. The foundation of the music collection was provided by a woman who sold Adda all of her original Beatles records, which she herself had bought as young woman and adoring fan in the 1960s.

Particularly curious finds are the editions of *Zéfiro* that Adda herself published some years ago. The instructional drawings on the art of lovemaking are seen in Brazil as a precursor to *Playboy*. Alcides Aguiar Caminha, a civil servant and father of five, published 500 erotic stories in comic form under the pseudonym Carlos Zéfiro and had become something of a legend of Brazilian eroticism from the 1940s to 1970s. His oeuvre is termed "erotic catechism." It wasn't until the beginning of the 1990s that his identity was uncovered in the Brazilian *Playboy*. You will find several editions in Adda's kiosk.

Address Rua Visconde de Pirajá, corner of Rua Maria Quitéria on Praça Nossa Senhora da Paz, Ipanema, Rio de Janeiro, RJ 22420-041 | **Getting there** Metro to General Osório | **Hours** Mon–Sat 10am–7pm | **Tip** The bar Barthodomeu (Rua Maria Quitéria 46, Rio de Janeiro, RJ 22410) serves delicious trifles and cold draft beer from noon until 3am.

2 — Angu do Gomes Bar
1950s' fast food

A little excursion to Largo de São Francisco da Prainha near the harbor is worthwhile even just to see the historical buildings that line the square, and the São Francisco da Prainha Church, built in 1696. It is here in the harbor that slaves arrived on ships from Africa (see ch. 104).

Before they were carted off to work in the gold mines or on the coffee plantations, they gathered on this square and made music full of homesick yearning on instruments they cobbled together. This was the genesis of samba. To this day, carnival groups still rehearse here months before their big performances.

This was also the place that Joel Gomes, son of Manoel, chose as the base station for his *Angu do Gomes*, which he produced on an almost industrial scale with 300 employees by 1977. Manoel Gomes has sold his specialty from little carts in the city center since the 1950s. *Angu do Gomes* was cheap, tasty, and very nutritious, perfect for refueling after a particularly long night. *Angu* is actually a kind of polenta, a soft mush made of corn or cassava flour, served with *vaca atolada*, which is literally "road-kill cow," but is in fact shredded ox ribs.

The carts with the fast food, served hot right through the night, soon became a regular, very democratic meeting place; artists, politicians, laborers, journalists, taxi drivers, and prostitutes would come face to face in the early hours of morning at one of the stalls. In the end, Gomes had over 40 carts, spread all around downtown.

In 1995, during the financial crisis, the restaurant temporarily closed, and Gomes once again concentrated purely on street sales. Now the *Angu do Gomes* is still prepared with the same recipe and served, hearty and delicious, in the new, beautifully renovated rooms of this iconic restaurant.

Address Rua Sacadura Cabral 75, Largo São Francisco da Prainha 17, Rio de Janeiro, RJ 20081-261, +55 (21) 2233-4561, www.angudogomes.com.br, angudogomes@angudogomes.com.br | **Getting there** Metro to Uruguaiana | **Hours** Mon–Thu 11am–10pm, Fri 11am–11pm, Sat 11am–6pm | **Tip** Marvel at the largest graffiti mural in Rio de Janeiro, on nearby Rua Coelho e Castro. Well-known artist Tomaz Viana painted the 1,200 square meters of wall space using 1,500 cans of paint.

3   Arataca Restaurant

Duck with toothache leaves

Proprietor Acir Rodriguez has lived in Rio for more than 60 years, and for more than 60 years he has hardly changed a thing in the interior of his restaurant. Just like you'd find in a grocery store in the Amazon region, cassava flour and distillates from his home in the state of Pará are lined up on the shelves.

Among the juices are *mangaba* and *murici*. The names come from the language of the Tupí-Guaraní Indians. *Murici* means "little tree," and the fruit is purported to have fever-lowering properties. Many of the foods from the Amazon are well known for their medicinal qualities, and the natives are usually closely connected with nature, healing illnesses using purely natural means.

Pato no tucupí (duck and *jambú* vegetables, cooked in *tucupí*) is one of the most delicious dishes on the menu. *Tucupí*, a cassava root extract containing hydrogen cyanide, which is detoxified by boiling it for a long time, lends the recipe its incomparable flavor. And *jambú* causes a surprising, tingling, slightly numbing feeling in the mouths of those with a European palate, which is why it is also called "toothache plant."

The same plant is also an ingredient in the native soup *tacacá*, which is served in a plain black bowl, in the original dish as it were, with dried shrimp, *goma* (tapioca starch), and a host of aromatic spices. It is widely available from street stalls in the Amazon and is supposed to work wonders for a hangover. For an extra punch, why not try *pimentão do cheiro* (literally: scented pepper), the "vinegar of the natives"?

Everything in the restaurant is authentic, as if you were in the Amazon. Many customers who are originally from the northeast come by at lunchtime for a bowl of *açaí*. The violet berry fruit compote is served ice cold with tapioca and contains many antioxidants, which is why health fanatics swear by it. It also happens to taste wonderful.

Address Rua Domingos Ferreira 41, Rio de Janeiro, RJ 22050-012, +55 (21) 2549-2076 | **Getting there** Metro to Siqueira Campos | **Hours** Daily 9am–9pm | **Tip** Nearby is a branch of the Brazilian cosmetic brand O Boticário, which produces natural products with tropical fragrances (Rua Santa Clara 70, Lojas A e B, Copacabana, Rio de Janeiro, RJ 22041-010, www.boticario.com.br).

4_ Atelier Brigadeiro Carioca

Sweet, creamy, divine!

The little balls of chocolate are sweet and delicious, but unfortunately, they are no good for your waistline – the ingredients are pure sin. *Brigadeiros*, traditional Brazilian bonbons, are made out of dark chocolate, sweetened condensed milk, and margarine, and then rolled in chocolate sprinkles. The sumptous little spheres, which taste a bit like chocolate truffles, are very popular as small desserts, snacks, and especially at children's birthday parties.

The name goes back to Eduardo Gomes, a major general, or *brigadeiro*, of the Brazilian Air Force, who ran for president in 1946 and 1950. His female fans – he was single and very good-looking – manufactured the little chocolate pralines in order to pour money into his election campaign coffers. It logically follows that the sweet temptations were christened *brigadeiros*.

In recent years, these confections have enjoyed a huge revival, and they are now a temptation in many cafés. In Atelier Brigadeiro Carioca, Flávio Fontoura and Renata Aragão have created a paradise for their happy childhood memories. They opened their first shop in the neighborhood of São Cristóvão and later began selling their sweets in the streets of the city center near Lapa from a small mobile vending cart.

Nowadays, they mostly fulfill custom orders, packaging individual *brigadeiros* in colorful wrappings. They offer over 30 different flavors of *brigadeiros* alongside the classic pure chocolate, including white chocolate, oats and honey, orange, coconut milk, caramel, Sicilian lemon, Nutella, pistachio, chestnut, and many more clever concoctions. Their popular specialty is called *Bem Casados* (the well-married), a rich chocolate bonbon with a *brigadeiro* in the middle. The chocolate globes in all their different guises are always the right consistency and always fresh. During the day, you can sample the range of the flavors at the vending cart in the city center.

Address Atelier Brigadeiro Carioca, Rua do Resende 11, Rio de Janeiro, RJ 20231-092, www.facebook.com/ateliebrigadeirocarioca | **Getting there** Metro to Carioca | **Hours** Mon–Fri noon–3pm, Sat 8am–noon | **Tip** The new, spectacular Museu do Amanhã, or the Museum of Tomorrow (Praça Mauá, 1, Rio de Janeiro, RJ 20081-240, www.museudoamanha.org.br), is worth a visit. Installations will take you, virtually, to the past, present, and future. With the help of a 360-degree perspective, you can experience the formation of the universe, for example, all within a few minutes.

5 Atelier Chamego Bonzolandia

The Bonzolandia family

Even though his work is now shown at international exhibitions and adorns the uniforms of Brazilian competitive cycling teams, artist and master upcycler Getúlio Damasio can still be found at work in his simple studio, known as Ateleier Chamego Bonzolandia, every day. He left his home in the state of Minas Gerais at the age of 15 in the hope of finding happiness here in Rio de Janeiro. He eked out a living by working different jobs, but he could never decide on one particular career.

His studio in an old wagon, similar to the historical Santa Teresa *bonde* (tram), is overflowing with his artworks, all made using recycled materials. Getúlio paints and builds new pieces of art relentlessly, adding a detail here or there, not stopping, even while he's talking to his customers or passersby. The bonde itself was his first recycling project, and it has been his workshop ever since.

One day, Getúlio had the idea of making puppets out of plastic bottle tops, slats from wooden crates, and metal sieves in order to earn a little extra money. People bought them – and now they have become his trademark. He gives each of them a name and the Bonzolandia family – in reference to his own – crop up time and again.

If you take a closer look at the sayings on the little works of art, you will find all kinds of philosophical musings. Under a crucifix, for example, is written: "Love is beautiful and costs nothing!"

Getúlio never rests. "I always think of something I could do with a plastic bottle or a piece of wood that no one needs anymore. Too much material is wasted as it is. At least I make something out of things that cost nothing – true love and passion aren't commercial projects. As an artist, you don't want to become rich. I can live off my art, which is fantastic. Many other people need a job to feed themselves. I don't, thank God."

Address Atelier Chamego Bonzolandia, Rua Leopoldo Fróis 15, Rio de Janeiro, RJ 20241-330 | **Getting there** Bus 5 or 6 to Rua Almirante Alexandrino próximo ao 35 | **Hours** Mon–Sat 9am–6pm | **Tip** One kilometer further on (Rua Paschoal Carlos Magno 124, Santa Teresa, Rio de Janeiro, RJ 20240), is Cultivar, a small café that serves the best pão de queijo (Brazilian cheese balls) in the city.

6_ The Babilônia Rio Hostel

High above the Copacabana beach

When Beatriz and Inês began plotting and scheming in the tele-novela *Babilônia* in 2015, the number of guests at the Babilônia Rio Hostel rose by about 40 percent. After all, the soap operas, three of which are broadcast every evening on the popular channel Rede Globo, are responsible for setting the main topics of discussion all over Brazil, including serious societal issues, and filming locations quickly become pilgrimage sites. Even kick off in the Brazilian soccer league has to wait until the last scenes of the soap operas have flickered across the country's screens. *Babilônia* is set in part in the eponymous, pacified *favela* above the neighborhood of Leme, near Copacabana.

Eduardo Figueiredo and his wife Bianca couldn't have wished for better publicity, and free at that. The couple had already de-cided to open a hostel for tourists in the Babilônia *favela* when, in the run-up to the huge sporting events in Rio, the 2014 World Cup and the 2016 Olympic Games, it became clear that the cost of accommodation in the neighborhoods by the beach, such as Co-pacabana and Ipanema would rise considerably, but that demand for cheap accommodation would remain. In any case, their view of the beaches of Leme and Copacabana is breathtaking, and es-pecially magical at dusk, when the lights on the Avenida Atlânti-ca begin to sparkle.

Eduardo and Bianca created the hostel with its six rooms by converting and renovating the house where Bianca was born. Color-ful graffiti, a common terrace, and a pool table all add to the relaxed ambience.

But the climbing wall that Eduardo had built is a pure extravagance. It is a testimony to his passion for climbing. In fact, before Eduardo became a hostel owner, he worked as an *alpinista industrial* (industrial climber) on an oil platform.

Address Babilônia Rio Hostel, Ladeira Ary Barroso 50, Leme, Rio de Janeiro, RJ 22010-060, +55 (21) 3873-6826, babiloniariohostel.com.br | **Getting there** Metro to Cardeal Arcoverde, then along Avenida Atlântica to Leme, via Rua Aurelino Leal at the restaurant La Foirentina to Ladera Ary Barroso, otherwise taxi from the metro station | **Tip** Bar Do Davide mixes delicious *caipirinhas* and prepares savory seafood (Ladeira Ary Barroso 66, Loja 03, Chapéu Mangueira, Rio de Janeiro, RJ 22010-020, www.facebook.com/BardoDavidOficial).

7 — Bar Brasil

Radical integration

Several large waves of German-speaking migrants have immigrated to Brazil with the hope of finding happiness in the New World. Many of the 34,624 ethnic German migrants documented in the recordbooks between 1907 and 1917 ended up opening restaurants serving specialties from back home. Among them were a group of Austrians, who established Bar Zeppelin on Avenida Mem de Sá in Rio de Janeiro in 1908. Pork knuckle with sauerkraut, Frankfurter sausages, smoked *Kassler* (pork), and ice-cold beer on the menu, were a recipe for resounding success.

But during World War II, when Brazil was the only South American country to fight on the side of the Allies against Nazi Germany (see ch. 98), any connection to the home country was shunned. The owners decided to take a radical step and unceremoniously renamed the place Bar Brasil. But to this day there is nothing much Brazilian about the fare on offer at Bar Brasil – the menu has hardly changed at all.

In the meantime, the bar, bang in the middle of the nightlife in the neighborhood of Lapa, has been taken over by two Spaniards. For a long time during the Bohemian heyday of the 1970s, Bar Brasil, together with Nova Capela, were the only bars in the neighborhood and often the setting of anarchic discussions that lasted into the early hours of morning.

Today, the place is rather peaceful when compared with all the music venues and bars that have popped up since Lapa's revival. But the *chope* (draft beer) is always ice cold, and many Cariocas think it's the best in the city – probably because it is cooled down to around zero degrees in a 60-meter-long pipeline before it comes out of the tap.

The interior décor is unchanged, and the wooden floor is still the same, as is the bar itself. A pleasant breeze continues to blow through the two doors, and a hint of Bohemian charm has survived, although nowadays the fun ends at midnight.

Address Avenida Mem de Sá 90, Lapa, Rio de Janeiro, RJ 2509-5943,
+55 (21) 2509-5943 | **Getting there** Metro to Cinelândia | **Hours** Mon–Fri
11:30am–midnight, Sat 11:30am–6pm | **Tip** The traditional bar Carioca da Gema
serves pizza, cold draught beer, and live music (Av. Mem de Sá 79, Rio de Janeiro,
RJ 20230-150, www.barcariocadagema.com.br).

8_ The Bhering Factory

Art cluster

The Bhering Factory produced high-quality chocolate in this location from the 1930s until the 1990s. The building then stood vacant until 2008, when Rui Baretto, a businessman in the instant coffee sector, purchased it – but only in order to buy the Globo coffee brand, which was contingent on purchasing the factory building as well. At over 80 years old, Baretto decided to dedicate himself ardently to the arts and turned the factory into an art space. The building itself is an architectural beauty. With almost 20,000 square meters of steel and concrete, this raw and imposing industrial building is bathed in the natural light provided by many glass windows originally from Hamburg and later transported to Rio.

A creative cluster of around 80 artists has settled into the space, which also makes it exciting for visitors. There are start-up companies registered here, such as Velt, which creates functional design at affordable prices. Others pursue the classical arts. Brigida de Murtas on the fifth floor restores oil paintings and creates *trompe l'œil* pieces of her own. You can visit sculptors absorbed in preparations for installations. René Machado, for example, works with mixed-media techniques, photos, and spray paints, inspired by everyday life in the city. Or pop in to see the photographer Paulo Salgado, whose photographic agency ICON Fotobrasil has its offices here.

Once a year, there is a party in the large hall for everyone, and the comic book publisher A Bolha holds its office party on the roof. This thrilling mixture of lively modern creativity and historical industrial charm attracts many event organizers too. The Rio Design Trade Fair regularly chooses the historical factory as the backdrop for exhibitions. Make sure you don't miss out on a visit to the café for delicious cake and chocolate, a nod to the building's history.

Address Fábrica Bhering, Rua Orestes 28, Santo Cristo, Rio de Janeiro, RJ 20220-070, +55 (21) 2213-0014, www.fabricabhering.com | **Getting there** VLT tram 1 to Grace Lamb then 10-minutes' walk | **Hours** Mon–Sat 2–6pm | **Tip** Bar do Omar (Rua Sara 114, Santo Cristo, Rio de Janeiro, RJ 20220-090, www.facebook.com/BarDoOmar) serves tasty snacks in a pleasant atmosphere with spectacular city views.

9_ The Big Ramos Pool
We, the people, go to the beach

If you're asking yourself why this beach has two shores, it's because it's actually a swimming pool – just in front of the actual beach in the north of the city. But the real beach has been so polluted that no one has really been able to bathe there for decades.

That was why the government of the State of Rio de Janeiro decided to treat the population of people living in the underserved parts of the city, far away from Copacabana and Ipanema, to a public pool with an area of, believe it or not, 26,000 square meters! It takes 30 million liters of filtered sea water to fill it.

"The Big Ramos Pool will have the cleanest water in the whole of Rio de Janeiro," was the promise at its opening in 2001. The concept was a resounding success: on a sunny weekend the bathing complex can expect around 30,000 guests on average.

Time and again there is dispute about the condition of the huge pool and the complex in the local press, as "some people" can't behave themselves, there's all sorts in the water, such as grilling skewers and condoms.

But visitors do have a lot of fun. The Petrobras Corporation is among the sponsors – the company's neighboring plants were, after all, substantially involved in the pollution of the seawater. The giant pool is regularly cleaned in a filtration process – the acute stench on the side of the bay comes from the polluted seawater.

Nevertheless, the atmosphere on the weekend is fantastic, with party music, the smell of BBQs, and lots of beer. The record attendance is 60,000 bathers on one weekend. Many children enjoy the opportunity to jump around in the water carefree. After all, this is not the open sea, and the water is only two meters deep, so the danger of drowning is much reduced.

The huge pool has already been the setting for several telenovelas, including *O Clone* on Rede Globo.

Address Piscinão do Ramos, Parque das Vizinhanças de Ramos, Avenida Guanabara, Ramos Maré, Rio de Janeiro, RJ 21030-080, +55 (21) 3104-6124 | **Getting there** Train from Central (platform 12) towards Saracuruna, Mon–Sat roughly every five minutes, less often at the weekend (www.supervia.com.br/servicos-supervia) to Penha, right-hand exit to the bus stop. Bus 940 to Ramos, then across the viaduct over Avenida Brasília, leaving Maré *favela* behind you to your left and continue walking straight on. When you reach the Club Naval sign, stay to the left and walk to the end. It's advised to go with a local guide: Carioca Ivo Korytowski offers English language tours into the neighborhood of Ramos and to the pool (ivokory@gmail.com). | **Tip** Not far off, in the small church of Nossa Senhora da Conceição, the remarkable painting of Holy Communion, *Cenacolo*, is on display. The view of Rio and Igreja da Penha from here is also magnificent (Rua Carvalho Moutinho 200, Ramos, Rio de Janeiro, RJ 21031-220).

10 — The Bird Cemetery

Only the priest is missing

A bird is depicted on the sign at the entrance, together with the line: "I sing in order to please my friends." And the twittering of birds is also the only thing you can hear – here in the only cemetery for birds in all of Brazil, probably even the only one in the entire world. With its 24 graves, which are all about the size of a shoebox, the place seems like a miniature version of the cemetery next door on the island of Paquetá.

A clergyman does not attend to the burials here, but the ritual has, by all means, its dignity, with its very personal eulogies for the dearly departed. The gravestones are inscribed with messages such as, "O pássaro abatido" (The fallen bird) or "O pouso do pássaro cansado" (Resting place of a tired bird).

On the wall, lines by Brazilian poets with birds as their central theme give the atmosphere of the place added integrity. "On my land palm trees grow, where the birds sing." It was the artists Pedro Bruno and Augusto Silva from Paquetá Island who designed the bird cemetery in the 1940s, and a bust at the entrance honors Pedro Bruno to this day. A pensioner of over 90 years, Theóphilo de Souza, became the cemetery's devoted caretaker. The authorities permitted him to build his home on the abandoned lot, and he continues to assist people who would like to bury their deceased birds here.

Once a woman even brought her parrot here from Minas Gerais, 1,000 kilometers away. She had lived with the bird for 25 years. Half a year later she came back to place some flowers on the bird's grave.

The burials are free, and there's enough space – one month after a burial there is already nothing left of the deceased, and the next bird is often even buried on the old ashes of an existing grave. An individual gravestone, on the other hand, costs quite a bit, but can also be arranged on request.

Address Cemitério de pássaros, Cemitério dos Pássaros, Rua Joaquim Manoel de Macedo, Ilha de Paquetá, Rio de Janeiro, RJ 20396-010 | **Getting there** Ferry to Ilha de Paquetá (sets sail from the ferry harbor in the center of Rio, Praca XV). The passage takes 70 minutes and costs around 4.50 euros. The ferry operates approximately every three hours between 5am and 11pm, check here for the schedule: www.barcas-sa.com.br | **Tip** The view from Mirante do Morro da Cruz on the tip of the island is stunning.

11__ The Biscoito Globo Factory

Savory or sweet?

The packaging has stayed the same for over 60 years. Beach vendors hawk them, calling: "Biscoito Globo! Salgado ou doce?" ("Savory or sweet?"), and although they have never printed a single advertising poster, there is no one in Rio who doesn't know the round, fluffy biscuit – here they enjoy cult status.

They are also *en vogue* in terms of nutritional science, but rather by coincidence, because when the recipe was invented in the 1950s, no one knew why being gluten-free might be worthwhile. The ingredients are as simple as the beach vendors' call: cassava starch (*polvilho*), milk, fat, and sugar or salt. When you bite into them, they taste light and fluffy.

The rings of dough are freshly baked every day exclusively in the factory in the city center. Only around 30 employees are responsible for production – and distribution. And this also works in a simple way: the biscuits are only available via a 20 by 50 centimeter opening in the grated factory door, in exchange for cash only. In the summertime, the street vendors queue up early in the morning just to get hold of 50 packets. Around 10,000 of them hit the streets every day, and then the baking begins again, their shelf life being only three to four days.

You can buy the iconic snack at kiosks too, but kiosk owners are dependent on "itinerates" who go to Rua do Senado on their behalf. The profit margin for the vendor is huge – the price at the factory is 0.90 real; on the beach, a packet will go for five reais. Vendors are the true, walking, talking commercials for the product, but their marketing doesn't cost the company a single cent.

Nowadays Biscoito Globo has competition on the beach from a company that sells *pao de quijo*, or cheese puffs. So the owners are striking out to old new shores, as they have begun selling the cult biscuit from Rio in São Paulo again, the recipe's actual birthplace.

BISCOITO GLOBO

50 UNIDADES	———	R$ 55,00
40 UNIDADES	———	R$ 44,00
25 UNIDADES	———	R$ 27,50
VALOR UNITÁRIO	———	R$

Address Fabrica Biscoito Globo, Rua do Senado 273, Rio de Janeiro, RJ 20231-005, www.biscoitoglobo.com.br | **Getting there** Metro to Carioca | **Tip** The art-nouveau building that stands out at house number 264 has been home to the Trade Union of Gastronomy and Hoteliers since the 1920s (Rua do Senado 264, Rio de Janeiro, RJ 20231-005, www.sindicatohoteleirorj.com.br).

12 The Bonde Museum

Of longing and nostalgia

A classic view of Rio de Janeiro on touristy postcards is the *bondinho*, or cable car, driving across the historic Carioca aqueduct. But in fact, the old tram is only rarely spotted there, rattling along at a maximum speed of 40 kilometers an hour. Operation of the tram was suspended after a tragic accident that led to the death of a tourist in 2011. When a part of the route was reopened in August 2015 after several years of restoration work, the Cariocas queued up for hours for a trip on the beloved *bonde*. The residents of Santa Teresa loved their old tram, which brought them up and down the hill of today's fashionable neighborhood cheaply or – for more daring individuals – even for free. Anyone could jump onto the tram en route and wouldn't have to pay, but the tram only stopped at official stops. With the new train, which now complies with common safety standards, hitching a ride is no longer possible.

The route to Santa Teresa is the last section of the once comprehensive tram network that is still served. The tram went into operation in 1877, the first in South America, and at the time still drawn by horses. Later, it was expanded to traverse large parts of the city, a symbol of urban growth. In the 1950s, the tram was the Cariocas' daily means of transport, but because of increasing automobile traffic, it was almost completely closed down in the second half of the 20th century.

A photo exhibition in the *Museu do Bonde*, or Tram Museum, partly also in English, documents the history and heyday of the *bonde*. There are also antique vehicles in original, miniature models, and conductor uniforms on display. There is a total of 300 exhibits, part of which are shown in a provisional place near the Carioca tram stop, featuring freight trams along with city maps that present the routes of the tram over various epochs. The museum maintains a very nostalgic piece of the city's history.

Address R. Lélio Gama, s/n at Estação Carioca next to the Petrobrás building | **Getting there** Metro to Carioca | **Tip** Livereria Cultura is a bookship in a former cinema, and it's a wonderful place to browse and soak up the special ambience there (Rua Sen. Dantas 45, Centro, Rio de Janeiro, RJ 20031-202, www.livrariacultura.com.br).

13 __ Botequim do Jóia

Friends forever

If you're not a regular, it can be very difficult to work out whom to place your order with at Botequim do Jóia. It is clear, however, that Dona Alaide, the elderly lady with the friendly smile who brings the plates and bottles to the tables, has supreme command; but then there is also the gentleman at the table by the door, who brings some dirty plates to the kitchen before returning to his table – and his beer.

Since owner Jóia died eight years ago, regulars have been happy to lend widow Alaide a hand. After all, no one wants anything to change here because it's so nice the way it is. The corner bar is located in a landmarked house in the middle of Rio Antigo. There has been a *botequim*, a neighborhood bar, here since 1909, when it was called Café e Bar Rio Paiva.

During a recent renovation, the posters on the walls were taken down carefully and then put back up again after the renovation. That most of them were already quite grubby doesn't seem to bother anyone. The poster of Botafogo football team, and also those of all the naked *Playboy* beauties, have once again returned to their places of honor on the wall. Joaquin Nunes da Silva, old Jóia, actually collected them – old-school garage charm. The bar's community blog calls it "exquisitely decadent."

Guests are particularly fond of the *paio afogado no feijão acompanhado de farofa de ovos*, a not particularly lean, but very tasty sausage with beans, *farofa* (cassava flour) and eggs. But the daily specials – which can be found listed on the blackboard on the door, as there is no menu – *carne ensoppada* (meat stew) or BBQ chicken, are also excellent.

The hardcore regulars like to arrive for happy hour in the early afternoon and then stay to the bitter end to immerse themselves in a bit of the Bohemian Rio de Janeiro lifestyle. The beer is always ice-cold, and there is a samba session on Friday afternoons.

Address Rua Júlia Lopes de Almeida, on the corner of Rua da Conceição, Centro, Rio de Janeiro, RJ 20080-060, blog of the friends of Botequim do Jóia at www.tretasdabaia.zip.net | **Getting there** Metro to Uruguaiana | **Hours** Mon–Fri noon–3pm | **Tip** The art museum MAR, only ten-minutes' walk away, is worth a visit (Praça Mauá 5, Rio de Janeiro, RJ 20081-240, www.museudeartedorio.org.br).

14 Boulevard 28 de Setembro
The musical pavement

The whole neighborhood of Vila Isabel appears to be completely devoted to music. Situated right next to Maracanã metro station on Praça Barão de Drummond, a life-size bronze sculpture of one of the foremost composers of Música Popular Brasileira (MPB), Noel Rosa, sits at a table, where he is being served by a waiter – a classic scene from the life of the bohemian who was born in 1910. This is the start of the Boulevard 28 de Setembro, which crosses right through Vila Isabel.

The area already had a reputation as the place to be for bohemians in the 20th century, and many other stars alongside Noel Rosa lived here. Noel's Vila Isabel was for 1930s' Rio de Janeiro what Ipanema represented in the 1960s.

It therefore follows that in 1965, on the occasion of the 400th anniversary of the city, the architect Orlando Magdalen had the idea of decorating Boulevard 28 de Setembro using a classical Portuguese mosaic paving technique, to represent the scores of the great samba songs in a black-and-white pattern.

He first suggested the project at a meeting of the local Lions Club, where it was immediately accepted with enthusiasm. The musician Almirante chose the songs that were to adorn the pavement of the boulevard. The compositions of the grand masters were expertly simplified so that the scores became practical for the purposes of this project. Rio de Janeiro's Municipal Cultural Department was also impressed and soon agreed to implement the plans.

The city's anthem, *Cidade Maravilhosa*, composed by André Filho and made famous as a samba song by Carmen Miranda, (interpreted here by Caetano Veloso, www.youtube.com/watch?v=2gFeSJtsgAU) is represented at the very beginning. In total, 20 scores are skillfully worked into the pavement.

Strolling along the boulevard, you can still sense the laid-back life-style of those heady days in the *botequims*, the local bars, in Vila Isabel.

Address Boulevard 28 de Setembro, Vila Isabel, Rio de Janeiro, RJ 2055-1031 | **Getting there** Metro to Maracanã, exit to Praça Barão de Drummond | **Hours** Unrestricted | **Tip** In the traditional bar, Petisco da Villa, the food is good and the atmosphere on Saturdays at the spontaneous samba sessions is always high-spirited (Avenida 28 de Setembro 238, Rio de Janeiro, RJ 20551-031, www.petiscodavila.com.br).

15 The Cagarras Islands

A prehistoric natural paradise

They can be made out in the distance from Ipanema beach and look like white rocks. Geologically, the seven Cagarras Islands date from the time when the southern hemisphere was one single continent. Millions of years ago they were part of a mountain ridge. At the end of the last ice age, the sea level rose and the mountains became islands.

The Cagarras Islands get their name from the vernacular, derived from the word *cagar* (to crap), in reference to the huge amount of excrement that sea birds leave behind on the islands. It is reputed that the calcium-rich feces has colored the islands white. Whether or not this is true, the fact remains this is a natural paradise for birds, which nest here in their thousands.

The archipelago is about seven nautical miles beyond Guanabara Bay off Rio's coast. The islands have never been inhabited by modern humans. For one, it is extremely difficult to land there, and there are also no freshwater springs. However, researchers have found the remains of human life on one of the islands. Before Pedro Cabral discovered Brazil, the Tupí Indians spent time on the island – but academics suspect this was only in order to celebrate rituals such as funerals.

The archipelago has been a protected nature reserve since 2010, so that this untouched ecological paradise can be studied and preserved. The native birds include gulls, snipes, owls, South American terns, cormorants, herons, magnificent frigatebirds, and even vultures. The seafloor bustles with many colorful fish such as Cuban hogfish and sea urchins. Green turtles have also been seen nearby on occasion.

You can take a boat trip to the islands and maybe even spot humpback whales and dolphins. From the sea, you will gain a new perspective of the stunning bay, including the Marina da Glória, Flamengo beach, Sugarloaf Mountain, the length of Copacabana to Arpoador. A breathtaking sight!

Address Cagarras Islands, Guanabara Bay, Rio de Janeiro | **Getting there** Arrange a four-hour tour (10am–2pm) to the islands on Sundays, departing from Marina da Glória boat trip via Saveiros Tours (Avenida Infante Dom Henrique, Lojas 13 and 14, Marina da Glória, Glória, Rio de Janeiro, RJ, CEP 20021-140 www.saveiros.com.br) | **Hours** Unrestricted from the ocean | **Tip** Mar do Rio organizes diving tours to the islands, as well as diving courses (Avenida Infante Dom Henrique, s/n Loja 16, Marina da Glória, Glória, Rio de Janeiro, RJ, CEP 20021-140, mardorio.com.br).

16 — Canal das Taxas

Snap!

Bumping into a 3.5-meter-long alligator on the street in the middle of the city is unusual, even in the tropics. The broad-snouted caiman live in the Canal das Taxas, right in the middle of the peaceful neighborhood of Recreio dos Bandeirantes, where middle-class families live. In general, the large reptiles swim around the canal languidly, and in the afternoon they like to lie in the sun. From the bridge, you can watch from a safe distance as their powerful bodies glide through the water.

But the canal is heavily polluted, and so occasionally one of the 30 crocodiles that live there will climb out in order to hunt for better food. These events are concerning. Now and then a caiman will slide into the swimming pool of some local residents, who will undoubted get the shock of their lives when they want to take a quick dip themselves before driving to the office in the morning. Sometimes, one will end up getting run over on the nearby highway Avenida das Américas – the reptiles find orientation difficult on asphalt and concrete.

Dr Ricardo Freitas Filho, biologist and founder of the Instituto Jacaré – Conservação e Manejo de Animais Silvestres, or the Caiman Institute – Preservation and Management of Wild Animals, does not believe that there are too many caimans in the lagoon complex, but rather that their natural habitat is being radically reduced by the rapid urbanization in the eastern part of the city. Put simply, this is the crocodile's home; if anyone should make way, then it should be the humans.

The crocodiles normally feed on crustaceans and fish as well as large birds and small mammals; they don't attack humans. However, they are not cuddly toys. The biologist strongly advises against feeding them. From the bridge you can sometimes quietly observe how one of the reptiles sneaks up on a particularly mouth-watering heron in slow motion and … snap!

Address Rua Mario Faustino, Recreio dos Bandeirantes, Rio de Janeiro, RJ 22795-225 |
Getting there Bus 2329 towards Castelo / Recreio dos Bandeirantes to Avenida Lúcio
Costa at Posto 10 or metro L1, L4 to Jardim Oceanico, then bus 2334 to Avenida das
Americas near Posto 10, then walk, after the restaurant Lokau, turn left into Rua
Marechal Olympio Falconiere and continue on to the bridge | **Hours** Unrestricted | **Tip**
Monika Gläsel Silva organizes environmental tours to see the caimans, including those in
the Chico Mendes Park, and also to see the sloths in Prainha Nature Park (see ch. 86).
Email moni-bra-tour@outlook.com to request information and to book a tour.

17__The Candle Palace

Which religion can I get you?

In summertime, the thermometer at Uruguaiana metro station often hits 40ºC/104ºF, and thoughts of the Sahara Desert are not far off. Sahara in Portuguese is Saara, which is also the name of the shopping district, officially named after SAARA, the Sociedade de Amigos das Adjacências da Rua da Alfândega, or the Society of Friends of Rua da Alfândega and Surroundings.

In this case, the word also refers to the busy streets to the east of Praça da República, which holds over 1,000 shops filled with copious amounts of anything and everything useful, decorative, chic, but most importantly, cheap – clothes, carnival accessories – feathers and sequins – shoes, including a lot of "Made in China" odds and ends. Even sex toys are advertised via loudspeaker. You'll feel more like you're in a Middle Eastern souk than in the bargain lane of a South American shopping center.

Many of the vendors are Syrians, Lebanese, Jews, Greeks, and Turks, who settled here more than a century ago. In 1962, the shop-owners in these 13 shopping streets joined forces and formed the SAARA organization. Immigrants and descendants from countries that are currently at war with one another live here together to peace without any religious dispute. Perhaps the diversity is simply too great for any conflicts to arise.

Many people who come to one of the shops, Palácio das Velas, or Candle Palace, are often looking for candles to decorate their homes – and the display window already provides the first chance to marvel at Madonnas and Orixás in every possible size from the Afro-Brazilian religions of Umbanda and Candomblé. If you're not familiar with these beliefs, it's easy to get confused. With over 1,000 holy figures, it's hard to keep track. Does Oxum, Goddess of Fertility, wear a yellow or a blue cloak? There are even sabre-swinging Saracens, dressed in all the colors of the rainbow. It's okay to ask for help.

Address Palácio das Velas, Rua Senhor dos Passos 104, Centro, Rio de Janeiro, RJ 20061-010, +55 (21) 3489-8648, www.palaciodasvelas.com.br | **Getting there** Metro to Uruguaiana | **Hours** Mon–Fri 9am–7:30pm, Sat 9am–3pm | **Tip** Sírio e Libanês Restaurant serves excellent Middle Eastern food (Rua Senhor dos Passos 217, Centro, Rio de Janeiro, RJ 20061-010, www.sirioelibanes.com.br).

18 Cardeal Arcoverde Metro Station

Antonio Veronese's "girls"

The great bossa-nova composer Tom Jobim said, "Among Antonio Veronese's pictures, there are beautiful women with whom, if I were single, I would happily fall in love," and he wrote these words on a sign on a wall inside a metro station in Copacabana.

The painter Antonio Veronese's beautiful women, which Jobim himself called *moças* (girls), adorn the gaps underneath stony archways that look like dark caves on the platform. The impressive works of art, four portraits of naked women, are a stark contrast to the rugged stone of the underground station, which lies 20 meters below sea level.

The metro station itself is a work of art and an adventurous architectural project. Passengers must walk 190 meters, or 623 feet, from the entrance to the platform. In order to make the long walk more pleasurable, the architect designed the passageways in different colors, from violet to green, with some elevators and paths in between. In this way, the impression of a long tunnel is avoided. Special drilling techniques were used in order to penetrate to a depth of 20 meters below sea level. In total, 200,000 cubic meters, over 700,000 cubic feet, of a gigantic granite rock face were removed.

The four *moças* have no names. The artist, born in the small town of Brotas near São Paulo in 1953, doesn't give any of his work titles, even if some gallery owners choose to ignore this and assign identifiers of their own. He also does not wish to explain his work. His painting is a silent, spontaneous act, and the results are always surprising.

"It is like making love: one never knows how it's going to end up." Veronese now lives in Paris, and his work is exhibited in many museums around the world. In Brazil he uses his art to combat child abuse, while his subway paintings continue to catch the eye of weary commuters each day.

Address Cardeal Arcoverde metro station | **Getting there** Metro to Cardeal Arcoverde | **Tip** You can see the drawing *Batcaverna* (*Batman of the Cave*) if you look up towards the highest point in the passage with the color panels, right after the escalator.

19 — The Carnival Block

We in Ramos will be Indians!

Among the residents of the neighborhood of Ramos in the north of Rio de Janeiro, middle-class families form the majority. It's a rather quiet area with lots of detached houses. On Sundays, many locals go to the local bar for a couple of beers and a game of cards with the neighbors.

It was on just such an afternoon in January 1961 when three samba-mad families from the neighborhood met and decided to start their own carnival group. The *blocos* are strictly limited to their district, in contrast to the samba schools that compete against each other city-wide in the carnival. Since the beginnings of samba, however, carnival groups have been fundamentally important to the development of the dance.

The enthusiastic group decided to christen their block Ramos Chieftains. Ubinary do Nacimento, one of the co-founders of the Chieftains, explains that the names of the founding families, all three of indigenous origin, gave them the idea of using a chieftain as the emblem for the group.

Every carnival group also has its very own theme song, which it plays over and over again as a kind of distinguishing identifier, in this case the eponymous "Cacique de Ramos," or "Ramos Chieftains," along with new compositions. For the street parade, of course, all of the members dress up as Indians too – every year. Comparable to a samba school, Cacique de Ramos brought together more than 10,000 members in the years when the parade still took place on Avenida Rio Branco. Since the official Carnival parades moved to the Sambódromo, or Sambadrome, the street parades have become less important. But the Chieftains are still one of the biggest and most popular groups in the city. If you want to see them dance during carnival, they traditionally march on the Avenida Rio Branco (meeting on the corner of Avenida Presidente Vargas.

Address Cacique de Ramos, Rua Uranos 1326, Olaria, Rio de Janeiro, RJ 21060-070, +55 (21) 98543-3821, www.caciquederamos.com.br | **Getting there** Train from Central (platform 12) to Olaria | **Hours** Sun from 5pm, Roda de Samba; visit the website for other events, for example the traditional *feijoada* meal | **Tip** Carioca Ivo Korytowski takes guided tours through the neighborhood of Ramos in English, dates on request at ivokory@gmail.com.

20 __ Casa da Tapioca
The best cassava crêpes

Time and again, the minibus driver is forced to crawl carefully round the tight bends because of oncoming trucks, which are fit to burst with construction materials. After the adventurous minibus journey, the last stretch has to be covered on foot.

The *favela* Vidigal has been in the grips of a construction boom for a long time now. Here, the gentrification of the formerly poor neighborhood is at its most advanced stage. A German real estate company had already tried its luck in 2009 with an investment of millions, and failed. In the meantime, Vidigal has become one of the hippest residential areas in Rio – several hundred foreigners already live here. After all, stunning scenery awaits at the top of the hill, with views of Leblon, Ipanema, Arpoador, and Sugarloaf. The Hotel do Mirante do Avrão offers spectacular views. For years, the sons and daughters from the ritzy neighborhoods have been coming to the legendary *baile funk* dance events on Saturday evenings, until quite recently a big hit in Bar da Laje, but there is no trace of the *favelados*, the area's former residents.

Casa da Tapioca is tucked in between the viewing terraces. This piece of land used to belong to Robert and Nubia from Pernambuco in northern Brazil, but now they only own the little house. They sold the land with its privileged positioning after the pacification of the *favela*, but Nubia continues to run their little shop successfully.

It's no surprise that the *tapiocas* are very well received, especially when there are things going on in the evening. The specialty from northeast Brazil, which are reminiscent of crêpes but made with cassava flour, come in sweet and savory varieties, all of them delicious. Chicken with *catupiry* (cream cheese), *carne seca* (jerky), cheese, or the sweet variety with cinnamon, banana, and sugar are all popular. The *brigadeiro do copo* (see ch. 4) is also unbeatable – as an extra dessert after dessert!

Address Rua Almeida Lima 88, Arvrão, Vidigal, Rio de Janeiro, RJ 22452-030, www.facebook.com/casadatapiocavidigal | **Getting there** Metro L 1, L 4 to Jardim de Alha, then motortaxi or walk to Praça dos Direitos Humanos, then up the hill with a minibus or motortaxi | **Hours** Daily 11am–10pm | **Tip** Hostel Alto Vidigal (Rua Armando de Almeida Lima 2, Rio de Janeiro, RJ 22452-030) offers rooms with stunning views and can be booked at www.gomio.com.

21 Catete Palace
The president's revolver

President Getúlio Vargas used a 32-caliber revolver to shoot himself in the heart on the morning of August 24, 1954. He could take no more. Ministers – and generals – had issued the "master of political brinkmanship" an ultimatum after allegations of corruption, mismanagement, and a failed assassination attempt on his harshest critic. Without the support of the military, Vargas saw no way out and made himself a martyr. "If the birds of prey demand blood and wish to continue to exploit the Brazilian people, then I will sacrifice my life," he wrote in his suicide note. The president's suicide almost triggered a national revolt, and his political opponents' plans didn't work out – Getúlio Vargas remained popular *post mortem*. Via his paternalistic regime, Vargas had created an industrial nation with trade unions and institutions, the Estado Novo (New State) during his 19 years in office. His administration established suffrage for women, a national pension, and health insurance.

In the end, Vargas' downfall was his autocratic style. He wanted to have his biggest foe, the journalist and politician Carlos Lacerda, "swept out of the way." But the assassination attempt failed, and he himself was pilloried as the instigator.

The revolver he used and the striped pajamas that Vargas was wearing in his final hour are on exhibit in the Museu da República (Museum of the Republic) in Palácio do Catete. Alongside these bizarre artifacts, you can also see the presidents' stately rooms. From 1897 until 1960, when Brasília became the capital, the palace was the seat of 18 heads of government.

A walk through the gardens, which stretch from the road right down to the beach, is charming. The Baroness of Nova Friburgo, wife of the coffee baron Antonio Clemente Pinto, who had the palace built as their residence, wanted to live both on the road as well as by the sea…

Address Rua do Catete 153, Rio de Janeiro, RJ 22220-000 | **Getting there** Metro to Catete, exit A | **Hours** Tue–Fri 10am–5pm, Sat, Sun, & holidays 2–6pm | **Tip** Enjoy works by contemporary Brazilian artists in the garden of Galeria do Lago in the museum.

22 CCC Dance School

Musical lunch break

It's over at 3pm, and everyone checks out, sweaty, laughing, and happy. The secretaries, lawyers, builders, and housewives have been dancing nonstop for two hours – now it's time to get back to work. The Baile do Meio Dia (Midday Dance), near the Praça Tiradentes in the city center, has been a regular meeting place for those in the know for over 10 years.

Anyone who wishes to succumb to the rhythm during lunch break on Fridays is welcome to come up to the third floor of the historic building of the Carioca Cultural Center (CCC) Dance School. Dances include the Forró from northeast Brazil, as well as the Bolero, Zouk, and Lambada – partner dance in all of its diversity.

Rosangela Pinhero has been a dance teacher for over 18 years. She says that the idea of using the lunch break to practice dancing actually came from her pupils, who wanted more time to practice. She herself also pops in now and then for a bit of a Friday lunchtime dance. She's happy to show you a couple of steps if you don't have any experience – at the end of the "lunch break" everyone will have tried at least one dance.

The Centro Cultural Carioca Dance School has been run by Isnard Manso since 1996. He had actually studied industrial design and originally worked for a multinational corporation: "But I was unhappy. I just wanted to dance!" When the music video for the song "Chorando Se Foi", with people dancing the Lambada on the dream beach of Trancoso in Bahía, went all around the world at the beginning of the 1990s, Isnard quit his job and dedicated himself solely to dancing. He's been the boss of the dance school since 1996 and also choreographs dances for the stage.

The Midday Dance is still an insider tip, but every now and again a stranger will stray inside, attracted by the music that blares out of the open windows. They are, of course, warmly welcomed.

Address Dança CCC, Rua Sete de Setembro 237, Praça Tiradentes, Rio de Janeiro, RJ 20060-010, +55 (21) 3176-1412, www.dancaccc.com.br, contato@dancaccc.com.br | **Getting there** Metro to Carioca | **Hours** Fri 12:30–5pm | **Tip** The equestrian statue of Emperor Dom Pedro I on Praça Tiradentes, with a height of almost 16 meters, is worth a look. The allegories on each side symbolize the fauna of Brazil, the indigenous people, and the country's major rivers: São Francisco, Madeira, Amazon, and Paraná.

23 — The Celebrity Cemetery

Carmen Miranda and friends

As a sports reporter, he was famous not only for his vocal acrobatics, but also because he commentated on games involving his favorite club, Flamengo, so passionately. Sometimes he would storm out of the commentator's box in order to celebrate a goal by his team pitch-side. Ary Evangelista Barroso died in 1964 and was also one of the most popular Brazilian composers and singers of the 1940s and 1950s. Many other bossa nova greats, such as Tom Jobim and Vinícius de Moraes, are buried alongside him at the São João Batista Cemetery.

There is the singer Clara Nunes, for example, whose songs are sung at her graveside by fans on the anniversary of her death. Or the film star Carmen Miranda, who died in Beverly Hills in 1955, but was transferred to her birthplace of Rio de Janeiro and buried here in the cemetery. Fans make regular pilgrimages to her grave.

The aviation pioneer Alberto Santos-Dumont is buried here; an imposing angel adorns his tomb. And a whole host of Brazilian politicians have also found their final resting places here, including no less than eight presidents.

But apart from the prominence of many who are buried here, a walk through the cemetery, with more than 100,000 graves, is like a stroll through an open-air museum. In the year 1852, Dom Pedro II inaugurated the first central cemetery of the city. Over two million people have now been laid to rest here, with over 100 elaborate mausoleums, including many designed by some of the country's most renowned artists in styles ranging from neoclassicism to modernism. The new cemetery administration is creating a map with names of famous people, descriptions of the artful gravestones, and biographies of the artists who designed them. Until that is available, savor the walkways and the art in silence, and look for the stunning views of *Christ the Redeemer* that are afforded in certain spots.

Address Cemitério São João Batista, Rua General Polidoro 222, Rio de Janeiro, RJ 22280-003 | **Getting there** Metro to Botafogo, then along Rua Voluntários da Pátria and left into Rua Dona Mariana to the entrance | **Hours** Daily 7am–5pm; once a month the historian Milton Teixeira gives a tour of the cemetery, which is almost like a journey through the history of Brazil (in Portuguese), dates at www.cemiteriosjb.com.br/#agendamento | **Tip** You can get a stunning view of Sugarloaf Mountain and the yacht harbor from Botafogo Praia Shopping Center (Praia de Botafogo 400, Botafogo, Rio de Janeiro, RJ 22250-040, www.botafogopraiashopping.com.br).

24　Chacrinha State Park

From Indio Teodoro to cheeky monkeys

Copacabana is never quiet. Some love life when it's lively, while for others, the constant hustle and bustle drives them crazy. If you're longing for a quiet spot, why not discover the 13 hectares/32 acres of untouched Atlantic Rainforest hidden here, right next to the Cardeal Arcoverde?

Local residents love Parque Estadual da Chacrinha, or Chacrinha State Park, especially those with children, who have the space to scamper around or celebrate birthday parties.

But the spacious area isn't just an outstanding playground. Kids also love feeding the adorable, common marmosets. Migrants from the northeast of Brazil originally brought the *Callitrichidae* to Rio as pets. Over the years, however, the tiny monkeys have spread out into many of the city's parks and are now even seen as something of a nuisance. Males are currently being chemically sterilized on a large scale. The delightful *micos*, which live in groups of two to 15 animals, aren't exactly shy.

A walk in the park is a bit like a mini-trek through the jungle, including some mysterious ruins to be discovered. The most famous is the oldest housing in Copacabana, where a fisherman named Teodoro lived in the 18th century – a simple hut of stone, earth, and seashells. He was apparently the only person who did not belong to the military to be tolerated here, in exchange for freshly caught fish. In the 1950s, it was decided that the military area would be converted into the nature reserve Parque da Chacrinha. People who had settled here in the meantime were expelled by the police in 1965. Today, the park welcomes its visitors with three paths that lead up to the peak, through lush vegetation with rare plant species, including the *Eugenia copacabanensis*, a type of myrtle named after the neighborhood. Otherwise there are marsupials, armadillos, owls … and lots and lots of tiny monkeys.

Address Parque da Chacrinha, Rua Guimarães Natal between Ladeira do Leme and Rua Assis Brasil, Rio de Janeiro, RJ 22011-090 | **Getting there** Metro to Cardeal Arcoverde, exit A to the left, then left past the gas station and follow the path to the entrance of the park | **Hours** Tue–Sun 8am–5pm | **Tip** Book well in advance for a guided walking tour through the park with magnificent viewing points. Ask for information at the entrance to the park.

25 __ The Chapel of the Souls
Where is the cross?

You arrive via the *Teleferica*, the cable car that has carried residents and visitors up to the 721-meter peak since 2015. The view of the harbor and the Niterói bridge is fantastic. Then go up the stairs to the plaza with the little church and children playing *futebol.* And another postcard panorama!

Morro da Providência was the first of the hills to be inhabited when soldiers returned from the bloody War of Canudos at the end of the 19th century. Brazilian governmental troops had brutally quelled a rebellion in Canudos in the state of Bahia, which had been under the leadership of the preacher Antônio Conselheiro. After their return home, they took up precarious accommodation here, while they waited for the minister of war to assign them dwellings. But that never happened. The settlement was christened Morro da Favela after the prickly plant that the soldiers had become acquainted with during the war in Bahia. Later, "*favela*" became synonymous with a poor community and the occupation of land without infrastructure.

If you walk up the little road on the right of the square, the alleyways become so narrow that they are reminiscent of a visit to a medieval village in Italy. There are many steps to climb up to reach the square with the mini church, the *Oratório.* The wives of the soldiers returning from the war in 1901 built the plain building for the "souls of the soldiers who didn't make it back home." The house of worship was originally adorned with a golden cross, but it was removed in the 1990s for restoration – and it was never returned. The church has been landmarked since 1986, but the restoration work has yet to be completed. In the meantime, 73-year-old Francisca Almeida looks after things inside and out. She has lived here on the square for 50 years and opens up the church for anyone interested in the cultural heritage of her neighborhood.

Address Morro da Provedencia, Rio de Janeiro, RJ 20220-290 | **Getting there** The Teleferica is not working at the moment; please contact your guide in advance and meet him at the meeting point (Central station, in front of Portoa no. 5). Generally, visit only with local guides, such as Provedencia Tourismo. Email felippsen19@hotmail.com for information and bookings. | **Tip** Right next to the cable car station, samba schools rehearse and march in the Cidade do Samba, or "Samba City" (R Rivadávia Corrêa 60, Gambôa, Rio de Janeiro, RJ 20220-290).

26 — Chapelaria Porto
Where did you get that hat?

The Panama hat is one of the most famous sartorial classics in the world. Ernest Hemingway wore one. So did Winston Churchill and Paul Newman. Originally, the straw hat protected Ecuadorian workers from the sun and is, in fact, an Ecuadorian invention. These hats are still made there by indigenous people using special palm leaves. But because they used to be imported into the USA via Panama, where they received their US-customs import stamp, they became known as Panama hats.

The elegant straw hat became famous when President Theodore Roosevelt donned one and drew the gaze of the international press on a visit to the building site of the Panama Canal in 1906. The hat enjoyed its Golden Age in Rio de Janeiro between 1930 and 1950. Anyone who was anyone couldn't be without one: the great samba composer Noel Rosa, President Getúlio Vargas, Tom Jobim, and many others. All of these celebrities had their hats made in Chapelaria Porto, which has been receiving customers at the same location near the harbor since 1880 before they moved downtown in 2016. Vanusa Damaso is now the fourth generation to hand-make hats to fit every head.

The building where the hat makers' factory now resides feels more like an office. But still Vanusa iss a master of her craft, which she in turn learned from her father Almir Romão Damaso, now 74.

If you like, you can have a hat made with your own personal touch, usually finished on the same day. Prices start at 130 reais, around 30 euros. The hat blanks are delivered to the Chapelaria from Ecuador in unfinished condition and then worked by hand by Vanusa to create the final product. A single hat can cost up to 1,000 euros (and fit comfortably in a matchbox) depending on the fineness of the material and the workmanship. To this day, many big *sambistas*, or samba dancers, order their hats at the old-school Chapelaria. Each Panama hat is as unique as its owner.

Address Avenida Presidente Vargas, 446 Sala 1703, Rio de Janeiro, RJ 20071-000, +55 (21) 2253-9605, or +55 (21) 99370-5615 (WhatsApp), www.facebook.com/ ChapelariaPortoll | **Getting there** Metro to Uruguaiana or Presidente Vargas | **Hours** Mon–Fri 9:30am–6pm, Sat 9:30am–3:30pm, please send WhatsApp in advance | **Tip** Trapiche Gamboa is a thrilling samba venue, offering shows, dancing, food, and drinks in a renovated warehouse (Tue–Fri from 6:30pm; Sat from 8:30pm; Rua Sacadura Cabral 155, Praça Mauá, Rio de Janeiro, RJ 20081-261, www.facebook.com/ trapichegamboaoficial).

27 — The Chopin Statue
Pieces of heaven

To enjoy the fantastic views from Pão de Açúcar, or Sugarloaf Mountain, you have to take the cable car 400 meters to the top. In a rush to get to the cable car station, most visitors will not notice the beach. But the small bay is enchanting, and Urca, with its architecturally interesting detached houses, is one of Rio's most charming – and safest – neighborhoods. The Military Institute of Engineering and the Military Academy have been based here since 1856.

Just in front of the beach stands a contemplative, two-and-a-half-meter-tall statue of Frédéric Chopin. The Polish community in Rio had the memorial built after German troops attacked Poland in September 1939, destroying the statue of the composer that had stood in Warsaw. The members of the community began to collect donations for a symbolic act of solidarity. In the very same year, the sculptor Augusto Zamoyski completed the new figure.

At the same time, however, the Brazilian government, although officially neutral as in World War I, nurtured sympathy for the German government, and the inauguration of the memorial was delayed. It wasn't until 1944, when Brazil declared war on the Axis powers after all (see ch. 98), that the statue was finally inaugurated on the Praça Floriano in front of the Municipal Theater. In 1960, Chopin had to make way for Brazil's most important Romantic composer Antônio Carlos Gom and ended up on Praia Vermelha, the "red beach." He fits in here perfectly, with his pensive pose, gazing out to sea.

In the evening, this area exudes a particularly welcoming atmosphere. Every Friday night, musicians from the Gruppo Movimento Artístico da Praia Vermelha cluster around the statue. From 9:30pm they play *choro*, a music genre that is in part influenced by Chopin's compositions. One of the most popular pieces, by Waldir Azevedo, is called "Pedacinhos do Céu," or "Pieces of Heaven."

Address Praia Vermelha, Urca, Rio de Janeiro, RJ 22290-270 | **Getting there** Metro to Botafogo, then bus 513 to Avenida Pasteur próximo ao 458 | **Hours** Unrestricted | **Tip** Urca, about 20-minutes' walk away, is a very popular bar for sunset aperitifs (R. Cândido Gafree 205, Rio de Janeiro, RJ 22291-080, www.barurca.com.br).

28_ The Church in Ipanema

Jesus was a surfer

He was a good person, and he surfed like a young god. Surely that must be more than enough to deserve canonization. At least that's how Guido Schäffer's loyal devotees see it. The shrine with his framed photograph on the left side of the Nossa Senhora da Paz Catholic Church clearly has the most flowers of any other altar and certainly the most believers kneeling in front of it.

His followers continue to worship him even though his canonization is far from guaranteed. The process has been going on for many years, and the Vatican only officially opened the case in January 2015. It could take some time, but the wait doesn't bother those who say their intercessions to Guido Schäffer. He died tragically in the prime of his life at the age of 34 during a surf trip. Although he was known as a top surfer on the beach at Ipanema, it was a wave that cost him his life.

Guido was actually a trained physician, but he later devoted himself to the spiritual life and wanted to become a Catholic priest. "The Lord called him into deeper waters for a more exalted life for Jesus," says his mother Maria Nazareth. "The sea fascinated him, not only in the sense of the great adventure, but rather to be closer to God, to discover the infinitude of heaven." He was about to complete his seminary studies to become a priest when he died. There were almost 2,000 people at his funeral ceremony. It was attended not only by sports enthusiasts, but also a great number of homeless people, whom Guido had assisted during his time as a doctor.

Those who knew him well know that he was a free person who also "had both feet on the ground," according to an episcopal advisor, who is convinced that the canonization is not far off. Until that happens, people pray to Guido without a papal blessing, offer him flowers, and ask him for small miracles – and even grand wonders.

Address Nossa Senhora da Paz, Rua Visconde de Pirajá 339, Ipanema, Rio de Janeiro, RJ 22410-003, +55 (21) 2523-4543 | **Getting there** Metro to General Osório | **Tip** The coconut ice cream at Sorvete Brasil (Rua Maria Quitéria 74, Ipanema, Rio de Janeiro, RJ 22411-002, www.sorvetebrasil.com.br) is particularly delicious.

29_ The Church of Saint Joseph

Behind the altar

The sight of the papier mâché altar figure of Saint Joseph, more than two meters high, is impressive. Surrounded by white flowers, he always appears festively decorated, as if every day were his special day.

There is little documented about this church, one of the oldest in the city, which appears quite plain from the outside, but baroque on the inside. All of the documents were lost in 1711 when the French plundered the city, including this church. What we do know is that a hermit consecrated a chapel to Saint Joseph here in 1608. The Brotherhood of Saint Joseph began work on the church, as it is to be found in the city center today, in 1807, and the dedication was in 1842. Rococo elements adorn the alcoves, some of them pieces by Simeão de Nazaré, a pupil of Mestre Valentim da Fonseca e Silva.

The couples who choose this church for their wedding ceremonies are enchanted by all its splendor. But that is all secondary to the devout – they come here to pray behind the magnificent altar.

You will observe this strange occurrence if you just sit for a moment and watch: one person after another will disappear behind the altar on the right, to reappear after some time on the other side.

What's back there? If you ask a Carioca they'll say: "See for yourself!" If you dare go behind the altar, you'll find a life-size Saint Joseph on his deathbed. To his right, Maria, to his left, Jesus as a grown man – a powerful image of Saint Joseph's achievements during his life. But what attracts believers so strongly to this place is its special energy.

Every believer experiences something different. Anecdotally, one woman was convinced that the feet of Saint Joseph were warm while she prayed. An art restorer working on the figure of Saint Joseph couldn't work alone because she felt the energy so powerfully. So go behind the altar and see for yourself!

Address Igreja São José, Avenida Presidente Antônio Carlos at the level of Rua São José, Rio de Janeiro, RJ 20010-010, +55 (21) 2533-4545 | **Getting there** Metro to Cinelandia or Carioca; VTL tram 2 to Praca XV | **Hours** Mon–Fri 8am–5pm | **Tip** Only about 300 meters away, one of the biggest art collections in Brazil awaits in the Museu Nacional de Belas Artes, in Avenida Rio Branco, with work by the greatest Brazilian masters of the 19th century (Victor Meireilles, Rodolfo Amoedo, Pedro Américo). Open Tue–Fri 10am–6pm; Sat, Sun, & holidays noon–6pm.

30 Cine Íris

Porn with a family tradition

Every morning at 10am, a member of the Cine Íris staff opens up the metal shutters with a stuttering clatter. Right in the center of Rio de Janeiro, in the legendary Rua da Carioca, the business of striptease and porn films opens for another day.

If you come and knock on the door half an hour earlier, you'll have the chance to soak up the ambience almost exclusively. And it hides some real architectural treasures. In fact, the old Cinematógrafo Soberano is the city's only art nouveau palace that is still completely preserved. The hand-painted Belgian ceramic tiles in the first story are a real rarity, as are the wrought-iron balconies and banisters. They were designed by the artist Antônio Borsoi, who was also responsible for the formidable Confeitaria Colombo.

The banisters still, to some extent, exude the flair of the great shows, when film premieres were regularly sold out. In the golden years of the theater, in the middle of the last century, shows and revues played here, musicals, lots of comedic material, some of which included thinly veiled social criticism.

Cine Íris has belonged to the Pimenta family since the beginning; third-generation Raul Pimenta manages it today. His grandfather and father look down on guests from the large portraits in the stairway. The guests, however, have changed somewhat over the course of the years.

In the 1970s, action films were popular, and since the 1980s the cinema has earned its money with porn films and live shows. The artistic director is a Portuguese language teacher, who becomes Lady Agatha in the 3:30pm show. Around 500 guests visited Cine Íris on its 100th birthday in 2014. Porn films made way for old musicals for the day, and the meter-high birthday cake was enjoyed by everyone. Despite the current subject matter, though, this movie palace retains much of its original splendor.

Address Rua da Carioca 49, Rio de Janeiro, RJ 20050-020, www.cineiris.com.br | **Getting there** Metro to Carioca | **Hours** Mon–Sat 10am–9:30pm, viewings between 9:30am & 10am | **Tip** You will find excellent Portuguese *pasteis de nata*, traditional custard tarts, in Casa Cavé, a café that has been in business since 1860 (Rua Sete de Setembro 137, Rio de Janeiro, RJ 20050-006, www.casacave.com.br).

31 Clube Renascença

When the sambistas have time off…

…they are back at the samba club at 4pm! More specifically, they are at Samba do Trabalhador (Samba of the Workers) in the neighborhood of Andaraí in the north of the city. The club started in 1951 with 50 or so people dancing each night. Today, up to 2,500 show up. When the BBC asked the boss for an interview, he thought: "Why are people from the land of the Beatles calling up and wanting to know about what's going on in Andaraí?" Here in the outskirts of town, everything is plain: the club is in an old sports hall; the basketball hoops still hang from the walls.

The venue has a first-class reputation among samba lovers. Famous musicians sit at the tables, with house singer and composer Moacyr Luz, who has written songs for Maria Bethânia, Nana Caymmi, and Gilberto Gil. He has composed music for telenovelas and written plays, and he wrote *Manual de Sobrevivência Nos Butiquins Mais Vagabundos* (*Manual for Surviving in the Most Abysmal Bars*).

Clube Renascença is a traditional meeting place to enjoy Samba de Raiz, or Roots Samba, a movement founded at the beginning of the 1950s by middle-class blacks as a place where they could express their cultural heritage in informal surroundings. At the time, they were excluded from white clubs. The management board is still made up of black people to this day.

The session kicks off at 4:30pm, and all of the tables are occupied by 6pm. Beer is sold by the plastic bucket, each containing 10 cans and brimming with ice. The music gets gradually louder and the mood better from the first to the third set. Moacyr greets an old lady warmly, and a professional dancer with a Panama hat cuts a rug on the dance floor. Soon, everyone is dancing. It is the combination of the old neighborhood, the enthusiastic crowd, the fantastic musicians, and the informal atmosphere that makes these samba evenings so much fun.

Address Samba do Trabalhador, Clube Renascença, Rua Barão de São Francisco 54, Andaraí, Rio de Janeiro, RJ 20560-032, +55 (21) 3253-2322, www.visit.rio/que_fazer/renascenca-clube | **Getting there** Metro to Uruguaiana, then via Rua Uruguia and Barao de Mesqita or by taxi | **Hours** Mon from 4:30pm | **Tip** The nearby Bar do Momo serves delicious *bolinho de arroz*, or rice balls (Rua General Espírito Santo Cardoso 50 A, Rio de Janeiro 20530-500, www.facebook.com/bardomomotijuca).

32 Cortiço da Lapa
Simple living

Senhora Edna Pinto lived in this courtyard for 52 years, until the year 2000. Her three sons grew up here, the oldest becoming a physician. In order to get to the kitchen, she had to cross the courtyard. Even the sink was outside.

The City of Rio de Janeiro has landmarked four of these types of complexes, not because of their architectural value, but for their historical importance. In 1886, 58 percent of the city's inhabitants lived in *cortiços*, simple collective living quarters. The characteristic living conditions were immortalized in the 1890 novel, *O Cortiço*, by Aluísio Azevedo. Brazilian naturalism in the Latin American context, the novel has been adapted twice for the Brazilian cinema screen.

One of the landmarked *cortiços* is Chora Vinagre. The accommodation mainly housed workers and employees, some of them Portuguese and Italian immigrants. In addition to daily routines and responsibilities, there was a lot of dancing and singing.

However, the dwellings also provided a refuge for disease and criminality – after all, everyone who lived here was poor. In order to curb the spread of disease, the building of new *cortiços* was later prohibited. Many houses, a lot of them *cortiços*, were demolished as part of Mayor Francisco Pereira Passos' (1902–1906) efforts to modernize the city. Programs such as Minha Casa Minha Vida, "My House, My Life," moved people out of the *cortices* and provided new accommodation for former tenants.

The *cortiço* in the middle of the Lapa neighborhood is the only one that is still occupied to this day, though some first-story rooms have been converted into a hostel. Robson Luiz, the manager of the residential complex, rents out six extremely plain rooms for people to enjoy this authentic atmosphere right in the center of the city. There are plans to make more rooms available once the current restoration work is complete.

Address Cortiço da Lapa, Rua dos Inválidos 124, Lapa, Rio de Janeiro, RJ 20231-000, +55 (21) 2224-9335, www.corticodalapa.com, ifazer@yahoo.com.br | **Tip** You can view another *cortiço* at Rua Senador Pompeu 43, Centro, Rio de Janeiro, RJ 20080-102, but only from outside.

33_ The Cradle Building

When Niemeyer still worked for free

During his 104 years on the planet, the exceptional architect designed the National Stadium in Rio de Janeiro, the United Nations Headquarters in New York City, and the famous Three Powers Plaza in Brasília. Oscar Niemeyer (1907 – 2012) realized over 600 unusual structures, many world-famous, which are known for their liquid forms and open design.

"I am attracted to free-flowing, sensual curves. The curves that I find in the mountains of my country, in the sinuousness of its rivers, in the waves of the ocean, and on the body of the beloved woman. Curves make up the entire universe." But the architect's passion for the curve only developed gradually over time.

In fact, nowadays you would hardly attribute the first project he completed on his own in 1937 to him at all. The Obra do Berço, which translates literally as "the cradle building," built as the headquarters for a philanthropic organization, appears rather inconspicuous, gray, and box-shaped, and it isn't in any way flowing or curved. But the *brise-soleil* technology, which the pioneering Swiss-French architect Le Corbusier originally designed as a sun protection system in Algeria and which Niemeyer had already used a year previously was also employed here. This time in vertical rather than horizontal form, it continues to work today, allowing the perfect regulation of daylight through the windows.

Unfortunately, the laborers executed Niemeyer's instructions incorrectly in his absence – he was on a trip abroad. Niemeyer couldn't and wouldn't accept the mistake, and he paid for the material costs of the new building himself. He designed the building without payment, and so he even ended up paying for the pleasure. Two years later, he traveled to New York with Lúcio Costa – with whom he later planned Brasília – to design the Brazilian pavilion for the 1964 World's Fair.

Address Obra do Berço, Rua Cícero Góis Monteiro 19, Lagoa, Rio de Janeiro, RJ 22471-240 | **Getting there** Bus 461, 473 from Copacabana to Avenida Epitacio Pessoa próximo ao 4866 | **Hours** Interior visits only with advance reservation at contato@aobradobercorj.org.br, Mon–Fri 8–10am & 2–4pm | **Tip** There is a cycle path around the Lagoa, and bikes are available for rent at several stations around the lake (www.bikerio.tembici.com.br).

34 Da Gema Corner Bar
Five-star standards in the outskirts

Four students from Rio's School of Gastonomy decided to go straight into action after graduation, opening a bar and serving hot food in their neighborhood. There were new dishes on offer – the newly minted young chefs wanted to show what they had learned from their training. The *pastel de feijão* (bean-filled pastry) was a tremendous hit. And the *lasanha de jiló* – a tiny, oven-baked lasagna with wafer-thin slices of crispy fried zucchini, *linguiça* smoked sausage, tomato sauce, and cheese on top, soon stormed the foodie columns of the big newspapers and magazines. It all began with an article in the gastronomy section of *Veja Rio* in 2012.

A move to a more ritzy area is out of the question, however. The effects of the financial crisis are still being felt in Brazil; everything is uncertain, and rents in better neighborhoods are exorbitant at the best of times. So the award-winning delicacies can still be enjoyed here in the rustic neighborhood of Tijuca.

The location is still the very same corner bar in which the four graduates began. Outside, cars and motorbikes continue to rattle past. Today, only two of them, Leonardo Amaral and Luisa Souza, are still involved. Their *coxinha de galinha* – a popular snack with chicken thighs, sometimes prepared and fried with palm hearts, other meats, or vegetables – is on the menu every Tuesday, and always fills the place.

The truth is, the bar is busy every day of the week. As there are always new creations among the *petiscos* (hot appetizers and snacks), the locals know that it's worth checking in every now and then. But guests also come from other neighborhoods in order to try the sophisticated *culinária carioca*. There are some really quirky concoctions among them such as polenta with cheese, allspice, and pork chops, or a black-bean cake that's creamy on the inside. The exciting culinary inventions just keep coming.

Address Rua Barão de Mesquita 615, Tijuca, Rio de Janeiro, RJ 20540-196,
+55 (21) 3549-1480, www.facebook.com/bardagema | **Hours** Tue–Thu 5pm–midnight,
Fri 5pm–2am, Sat 1pm–2am, Sun 1–7pm | **Tip** Dilma Rousseff, former president of
Brazil (2011 until her removal from office in 2016) was jailed and tortured just around
the corner at 1º Batalhão da Polícia do Exército, or 1st Batallion of the Military Police
(Rua Barão de Mesquita 425, Rio de Janeiro, RJ 20540-001) from 1970 to 1972 during
the military dictatorship. The building can only be viewed from the outside.

35 Despina Culture Loft
Inspired by Rio

For one, the Despina Culture Loft itself is worth seeing from a historical point of view: a loft in a venerable palace from the 19th century in the middle of downtown Rio and near the famous historical library, Real Gabinete Português de Leitura, or the Royal Portuguese Reading Room. The windows look out onto the atmospheric square and the São Francisco de Paula Church. Secondly, the Largo das Artes, or Arts Square, concept is ambitious and avant-garde, as local artist studios thrive alongside artist-in-residence ateliers, in which artists from all over the world have the opportunity to become inspired by the city – both historically as well as contemporarily.

The young artists come, for example, from The Netherlands, like Risja Steeghs, who works with collages, or from Helsingør in Denmark, like Marina Pagh, who has already worked in Tanzania and Japan and is known for her installations. Every month, two international artists arrive to work in the ateliers here and to enjoy the continuous exchange of ideas with other artists. At the end of their residency, they are invited to exhibit the works they have produced during their time in Rio.

The name Despina comes from one of the cities in Italo Calvino's book, *Invisible Cities*, which looks different depending on how you approach it, essentially taking on the form and perspective of the viewer.

The works of art to be featured are selected by curators for specific exhibitions and projects and thus placed in a critical context. The exhibitions are accompanied by events, debates, and discussions with the artists. One of the aims of the Despina Culture Loft is to reinvigorate the artistic and creative energy of the historic city center. For the visitor, it is an opportunity to see unique exhibitions and to get to know artists in person who are inspired to create new works of art in Rio Antigo, the Old City.

Address Largo das Artes, Rua Luís de Camões 2, Rio de Janeiro, RJ 20051-020, www.despina.org, info@despina.org | **Getting there** Metro to Uruguaiana or Carioca | **Hours** Mon–Fri 10am–7pm | **Tip** The historic Real Gabinete Português de Leitura, or Royal Portuguese Reading Room, is one of the most remarkable libraries in the world and worth a visit (Rua Luís de Camões 30, Centro, Rio de Janeiro, RJ 20051-020, Mon–Fri 9am–6pm, www.realgabinete.com.br).

36 DJ School Spin Rocinha
Professional sounds in the favela

Its pupils include 13-year-old student André and 55-year-old porter Robson. Twice a week from 7 to 9pm, Zezinho, born Renato da Silva, teaches the musical skills that get people moving at festivals and parties, presenting the art of loops and samples to anyone who is interested.

He is himself a native *favela* inhabitant, born and bred in Rocinha. His father was originally from northeast Brazil, and his mother is American. He lived in San Francisco for eight years, where he worked as a DJ and graffiti artist before moving on to Canada for a period of time. But it is Rocinha and the big heartedness of the residents that really makes him feel at home. With over 350,000 inhabitants, it is the biggest *favela* in the whole of Brazil. A van picks you up and drives you through the narrow winding streets from Ipanema, you only get a clear sense of the gigantic scale of this *favela* on the drive back down towards the valley on the other side of the mountain.

The stairs up to Zezinho's studio are steep, the décor is simple, but the DJ equipment, on the other hand, is highly professional – the equivalent of around 10,000 euros is invested in his audio hardware. The electro beats and house compositions seem to please the housemates, his three cats. Lessons from the professional are free for anyone and everyone. How long individuals stick with it is another question. At least one or two *favela* kids have managed to make it pay, getting jobs spinning disks at big parties, and working as professional DJs. For a gig in Rocinha they earn between 200 and 500 reais, in other neighborhoods 500 (currently around 150 USD) is the minimum. Zezinho finances the school with his tours through the *favela*, always ending with a visit to Spin Rocinha. His big dream is to create a culture center in Rocinha with lots of creative activities – not just music. He is already saving up.

Address Spin Rocinha, Estrada da Gavea 474, Apto. 301, Rio de Janeiro, RJ 22451-971, +55 (21) 98221-5572, www.spinrocinha.jimdo.com; reserve tours at www.favelatour.org | **Getting there** Van from Posto 10 into Rocinha (on a tour you will be picked up here) | **Tip** Trapia Social is a restaurant in Rocinha that serves an impressive array of delicious and filling foods (Travessa Liberdade do Bairro Barcellos 3, Via Apia, Rocinha, Rio de Janeiro, RJ 22451-460).

37 __Eduardo Guinle Park
Apartments for the elite

Anyone living in these apartments must have hit the jackpot! Originally, only Dr Eduardo Guinle's country house stood on these 25,000 square meters/6 acres of parkland. Today, three apartment buildings rise up on the right-hand side, designed by none other than Lúcio Costa, who planned the modernist capital Brasília with Oscar Niemeyer.

The structures are oriented towards the West, following the course of the park, and the *brise-soleil* façade elements regulate the rays of the sun and thus the temperatures inside the buildings. The playful use of the materials on the façade – ornamental tiles, vertical slats, and ceramic modules – is fascinating.

Originally, six residential buildings were planned for the complex, but only three were built. They were completed in 1948, 1950, and 1952, respectively, and conceived as luxury living spaces for members of the elite class. The apartments in the middle of the beautiful neighborhood of Laranjeiras range from 286 to 604 square meters (3,000 to 6,500 square feet) in size. Costa followed Le Corbusier's formal language, as evidenced in the use of pillars.

The park was originally laid out as the garden of the illustrious Guinle family's manor in the 1920s – son Octávio later built the Copacabana Palace Hotel. In 1940, the government took over the park, and Costa, as the director of the National Institute for Historic and Artistic Heritage from 1943, managed the urban planning and design.

Originally created to plans by the French landscape architect Gérard Coch and with elements by Burle Marx, the idyllic park, with its pond, ducks, geese, a children's playground with shady trees and tropical plants, is now landmarked and open to the public. Anyone who needs a little break from the hustle and bustle of the city streets is welcome to take a stroll and appreciate the architectural highlights and natural beauty.

Address Parque Eduardo Guinle, Rua Gago Coutinho 66, Laranjeiras, Rio de Janeiro, RJ 22221-070 | Getting there Metro to Largo do Machado | Tip Rotisseria Sírio-Libanesa in the Galeria Condor, just next to the metro station, has what may be the best *kibe*, or Lebanese croquettes, in the city (Largo do Machado 29, Catete, Rio de Janeiro, RJ 22221-020).

38 Esteves General Store

Where the great train robber bought his beer

Santa Teresa is one of the prettiest neighborhoods in the city. Colonial-style villas line the streets, and bars and cafés invite you to enjoy life. Artists, musicians, journalists, and Bohemians have lived here since the 1980s.

A notorious resident in the 1990s, until he returned to the UK in 2001, was Ronald Biggs, who had been involved, along with 14 accomplices, in the Great Train Robbery in England in 1963. The loot amounted to £2.6 million, equal to US$61 million in today's currency. The perpetrators were caught, but Biggs escaped after 15 months in jail. He went into hiding in Australia, among other places, and he finally ended up in Brazil, where he had a son with a Brazilian woman. This protected him from extradition, and the stolen millions were never to be recovered.

"He always paid his debts. He organized parties. He threw the biggest one on the 30th anniversary of the Great Train Robbery – with 30 cases of beer. He always invited everyone to his house and his swimming pool," neighbor Ricardo Esteves remembers. "He would sell 'I was in Rio and met Ronald Biggs' T-shirts to tourists, and he would then pay his bills with that money, within no more than three days."

The Esteves family, immigrants from Portugal, have run the Mercearia Estevez, which basically means "general store," since 1962. Biggs was a regular customer. The store's layout is simple; there's bread, ham, toothpaste, and the like on sale. You can even drink a can of beer and chat with the neighbors at the counter. Ronnie Biggs loved this simple life, and the shop hasn't changed a bit to this day.

"He was good natured and proud that he hadn't fired a single shot. He liked taking his dog for a walk and drank lots of beer and whiskey." Biggs recorded the song "No One Is Innocent" with the Sex Pistols, and when he died, aged 84, the Hells Angels paid their respects at his funeral.

Address Mercearia do Esteves, Rua Áurea 2, Santa Teresa, Rio de Janeiro, RJ 20240-210 | **Getting there** Bus 7 towards San Silvestre to Rua Paschoal Carlos Magno próximo ao 99 | **Hours** Daily 7:30am–8pm | **Tip** Ronald Biggs' home is just a short walk up the hill (Rua Monte Alegre 470, Larajeiras, Rio de Janeiro, RJ 20240-193).

39__ The Etnias Mural

Olympic street art

This homage to the 2016 Olympic Games by the Brazilian artist Carlos Eduardo Fernandes, alias Eduardo Kobra, is around 190 meters long and 15.5 meters tall.

Referencing the five Olympic Rings, the mural shows the faces of five people, each representing indigenous ethnic groups from the five continents, wearing traditional clothing: Asia is represented by a member of the Karen people from Thailand and Burma, Oceania by a Huli from Papua New Guinea, America by a Tapajó from the Amazonian rainforest, Africa by a Mursi from Ethiopia, and Europe by a Chukchi Eskimo from Siberia. The idea behind it was this simple concept: "We are all one!" The huge mural in the newly-gentrified harbor district was sponsored by the Rio 2016 Organisation Committee and Rio de Janeiro City Council.

Kobra, Brazil's most famous graffiti artist, has already completed several impressive murals in many of the world's major cities, including Paris, London, Dubai, and Tokyo, as well as other cities in Brazil. His most famous work to date is *Sailor Kiss* from 2013, visible from New York's High Line Elevated Park, which is a remake of a well-known post-war photographic motif: a sailor kissing a nurse on New York's Times Square in 1945.

It took Kobra and his team of four around two months to complete the 3,000-square-meter image on the exterior wall of a two-story warehouse near the refurbished Praça Mauá. The graffiti artists were busy for at least 12 hours every day. The artist always works with kaleidoscopic colors, composing his images using squares and triangles.

Around 380 liters of white paint, 1,500 liters of colored paint and at least 3,500 spray cans were used to create the gigantic work of art. It is now officially the largest graffiti in the world painted by a team – confirmed by its recent inclusion in the *Guinness Book of World Records*.

Address Etnias by Eduardo Kobra, Boulevard Olímpico, www.eduardokobra.com | **Getting there** VLT tram to Parada dos Museus, then two minutes' walk. | **Hours** Unrestricted from the outside | **Tip** *Saudade é amor, te sigo esperando* (*Longing is love, I follow you waiting*), a mural about a sailor's love by artist Rita, is also on Boulevard Olímpic.

40__ The Evictions Museum

"No one can evict memory"

Reports of how the inhabitants of the Vila Autódromo *favela* were resisting eviction went around the world in the runup to the 2016 Olympic Games, with articles published in newspapers from *The Guardian* to *The New York Times*. Many people could produce written guarantees stating a right of residency for 99 years, and the winner of the competition to build the Olympic Village had originally agreed to leave the *favela* untouched. Yet the City Council decided instead to clear out the settlement completely. However, 20 families resisted and were successful in having new apartments built for them in the same location.

More than 800 families had lived here peacefully for 50 years, from the time when it was swampland. The swanky Barra da Tijuca has grown up around the lagoon over the course of the decades, with skyscrapers and shopping centers (see Península Residential Area in ch. 109). In the end, Vila Autódromo was simply in the way of the Olympic Village.

The open-air Museu das Remoções (Evictions Museum) opened in May 2016. Homage is paid to people who were prominent in the struggle, such as its icon Maria da Penha Macena, in the form of sculptures made by architecture students. Apart from solitary relics, such as the electric meter from Dona Denise's house, the only thing left standing is the Catholic Church – everything else fell victim to the bulldozers.

On International Museum Day 2017, the archive material was received by the National Museum and will be accessible there in the future. Maria da Penha presented the concept of the museum with the words, "The fight goes on." It will be a memorial to the citizens of Vila Autódromo and for everyone who has been displaced, as a living archive: "No one can evict memory." In total, around 77,000 people lost their homes in the course of the Olympic Games and the soccer World Cup two years previous in Rio de Janeiro.

Address Museu das Remoções, Rua Vila Autódromo s/nº, Vila Autódromo, Barra da Tijuca, 22775-080 Rio de Janeiro | **Getting there** Metro to Jardim Oceânico, then BRT to Centro Olímpico, next to the Residence Inn by Marriott Rio | **Hours** Visit and guided tour led by a former *favela* inhabitant are possible by appointment, Whatsap Luiz +55 (21) 9990-9003, Sandra Maria +55 (21) 99675-2358 or email museudasremocoes@gmail.com | **Tip** The Parque Olímpico do Rio de Janeiro, or the 2016 Olympic Park, is only 15 minutes away and is open between 8am and 6pm (Av. Embaixador Abelardo Bueno 3401, Barra da Tijuca, Rio de Janeiro, RJ 22775-040, www.rio.rj.gov.br/web/secpar/parque-olimpico).

41 Extra Boulevard

Department store in a swanky factory hall

The entrance to this shopping center, with chandeliers on the ceiling, marble floors, and curved staircases, offers its visitors an opulent reception. The magnificent, 19th-century building was once a textile factory. The chimney is still visible from far off, and the workers' apartments in the neighboring streets are also preserved.

From the outside, the opulent brick building looks like a factory in England from the same period. The factory was in operation until 1960. After much renovation, it reopened in 1978 as a shining new shopping mall. European specialists were brought in to repair the builiding's decorative wrought-iron elements, such as the windows and the stairs. Looking down from the top floor, you get a real sense of the immensity of the factory. Four hundred mechanical looms were in use in 1885; by 1905 the number was already 1,600. The factory building may have been smartened up, but the workers' houses are still, as they were back then, in modest condition. This low-income housing, once for the employees of the factory, is still reserved for working-class, low-income families.

The Companhia de Fiação e Tecidos Confiança Industrial (the Industrial Spinning and Weaving Trust Company) is a milestone not only in the industrialization of Brazil, but also in the history of labor and the unions. The general strike of 1918 secured its place in the history books when 1,900 workers paralyzed the factory's operation. The Trust experienced its heyday during World War II, when it produced fabric for the Brazilian Army's uniforms – even the workers benefited from the rich profits of the time.

The factory was musically immortalized in a song by the great composer Noel Rosa, who lived in the neighborhood of Vila Isabel and was inspired to write one of his most well-known songs, "Três Apitos" ("Three Whistles"), by the daily sounding of the factory whistle.

Address Extra Boulevard Shopping, Rua Maxwell 300, Rio de Janeiro, RJ 20541-971, +55 (11) 3886-3164 | **Getting there** Metro to Saens Peña, then taxi, or metro to Estação Maracanã (and then taxi) | **Tip** There are many steps up to the Santo Antônio Church, but the panoramic view is worth all the effort (Igreja Santo Antônio, Rua Teodoro da Silva, Rio de Janeiro, RJ 20510-010).

42 The Farm Flagship Store

Colorful, quirky, Carioca!

Today the flagship stores of the brand Farm are palaces – more like event venues than fashion boutiques. But it all began very modestly. The creations by designers Marcello Bastos and Kátia Barros – with a hint of hippy romanticism, quirky prints, and colors – were a real surprise in 1997 when they hit the racks at the Babilônia Feira Hype, a monthly market that offers a stage for young and alternative labels in the city to showcase their designs. Within less than six months, the Farm stand was a big hit. The new objects of desire were bodysuits, printed skirts, and T-shirts. It was the fresh nonchalance, the colorful contrast to the rather dark and drab fashions of the time, that was immediately striking. Kátia Barros' great passion is carnival, and the song "Girl from Ipanema" is said to have inspired her designs.

Two years after their premiere at the alternative market, the two designers opened their first shop. The designs first conquered the chic Zona Sul of Rio de Janeiro on the beaches of Ipanema and Copacabana, then the whole of Brazil. Like no others, the two designers have managed to interpret and transport the authentic laid-back feeling of the beaches of Rio.

Today, the label enjoys cult status in Brazil. Some 32,500 items were sold on the first day after the presentation of the fall collection in 2008. The upward trend hasn't wavered since then. Not long after the first shop in Barcelona was opened, others in Europe followed. Today the brand sells everything you need for the "Brazilian lifestyle" and a relaxing day on the beach: dresses, accessories, bikinis, shoes, surfboards, bikes…

Farm is now a distinctive, uniform image, from the architectural design in the furnishings of the shops to the online store, and social networks. The youthfulness and coolness of the brand reflect the Rio lifestyle. Visiting the flagship store in Ipanema is a must.

Address Farm, Rua Visconde de Pirajá 365, Ipanema, Rio de Janeiro, RJ 22410-003, +55 (21) 3813-3817, www.farmrio.com.br | **Getting there** Metro to General Osório | **Hours** Mon–Fri 9am–9pm, Sat 9am–7pm, Sun noon–6pm | **Tip** Enjoy a superb rib-eye steak or filet at the nearby L'Entrecôte de Paris (Rua Prudente de Morais 1387, Ipanema, Rio de Janeiro, RJ 22420-043, www.lentrecotedeparis.com.br/rj-ipanema).

43 _ The Favela Museum
The history painter

From Mirante da Paz, or Viewing Point of Peace (see ch. 87), the path winds up through narrow alleyways and lots of stairs into the *favela* Cantagalo, which translates as "Cockcrow" and is so named as many of the inhabitants set off for work at dawn, down to Ipanema and Copacabana, as housemaids, sales assistants, mobile beach vendors, or caretakers.

Officially, around 20,000 people live in Cantagalo and the neighboring *favelas* of Pavão and Pavãozinho, which translate as "Peacock" and "Little Peacock." The association of beautiful birds with a slum is actually appropriate, as these *favelas* have produced several important artists. One of them is Acme, who brought the Museu de Favela, or MUF, to life with some friends in 2009 in order to break down prejudices, such as "only drug dealers and gangsters live here." The Favela Museum does have its own building, but most impressive is the *favela* itself as an "open-air museum."

"Casa Telas," or Canvas Houses, is the name of the project, which is made up of 25 murals that tell some of the stories of the *favela*. And Acme, born Carlos Esquivel, is the unofficial historian, or the painter of history. His images create memory. They tell the stories of the immigrants who came here over 40 years ago, of their dreams, most of which were crushed, and of the difficulties of life in the *favela*. "A woman with a canister on her head" reminds us that up until the middle of the 1980s, every single drop of water had to be carried up the steep steps from the posh neighborhood of Ipanema. Or they tell of the times when the bosses of the drugs cartels called all the shots, and many lost their lives in gunfights. The graffiti artwork, *Justiça Douglas DG*, is dedicated to Acme's friend, who was killed by the "Police Pacification Unit" (UPP).

Isabell Erdmann's guided tours take in the murals and introduce visitors to some of the locals.

Address Casa Telas, R. Nossa Sra. de Fátima 7, Ipanema, Rio de Janeiro, RJ 22071-060, +55 (21) 2267-6374, www.museudefavela.org/favelatour/english.html | Getting there Metro to General Osório | Hours The exhibits are in the streets, so visit only with a local guide, Isabell Erdmann, four hours and many stairs, at tourguiderio.jimdo.com | Tip Dona Rose's snacks in Bar da Bica (Rua Ari Barroso 24, Cantagalo, Rio de Janeiro, RJ 25805-060) are great for a delicious pit stop.

44__ The Feast of Iemanjá
Offerings for the goddess of the sea

She wears a silver crown and holds a silver fan in her hand. She is motherly, but also vain and not averse to luxury. Her colors are white, light blue, and pink. On February 2, Iemanjá, the goddess of the sea, is venerated as the mother of Orixá spirits. In Umbanda, a religion with African and Catholic elements, she is the equivalent of the Nossa Senhora da Conceição, "Our Lady of the Immaculate Conception." Not only does Iemanjá rule the waves of the sea, but of all bodies of water, as well as being the patron saint of the seamen and fishermen.

It is mainly followers of Umbanda – estimated at around 500,000 in Brazil, but possibly many more – who make their way down to the sea in the morning to bring their offerings to the goddess. There are several processions through the city on this day. The Congregação Espírita Umbandista do Brasil (CEUB) starts in the neighborhood of Estácio in the city center and is accompanied by hymns and chants. A four-meter-long boat full of offerings is carried right through the city center and then given over to the ocean in order to please the queen of the sea.

The goddess of fertility loves gifts! If she accepts the offerings – i.e. the sea doesn't wash them back up onto the beach – the giver's wish will be fulfilled. If not, they say, then the goddess has rejected them. It's not important whether you are fundamentally a believer –the main thing is that the wish is expressed in faith.

Hundreds of people pay homage to the goddess of the sea in long white robes, many of them with turbans on their heads. Along with lots of flowers, perfume (preferably lavender), dolls, combs, and make-up utensils are also accepted – in fact anything that a woman might need to make herself beautiful will do. Many Cariocas also dress up in white on December 31 and give the goddess of the sea white flowers for good luck.

Address Copacabana Posto 3 or, if you wish to follow the whole procession, from Estácio at around 8am, information at www.ceubrio.com.br or at Praça Cinelândia | **Getting there** Metro to Siqueira Campos or Cardeal Arcoverde | **Hours** Procession generally begins at 5pm | **Tip** It is worth popping into the quaint Botequim Informal for a drink (Avenida Nossa Senhora de Copacabana 434, Copacabana, Rio de Janeiro, RJ 22010-121, www.botequiminformal.com.br).

45 — The Feast of Saint George

A winner for all

São Jorge, or Saint George, is ranked number one on the list of the most popular tattoos in Rio, and people named Jorge always raise a toast to their namesake before every glass of cachaça they drink: "The holy soldier drinks with us!" His image graces many doorways, as he protects the home. The patron saint of the heart is Jorge, even if Sebastian is the official patron of the city.

His feast day is on April 23, a public holiday in Rio. People begin to queue up in front of the St George Church hours before early mass begins. The garb of the devotees is uniform – bankers, builders, housewives, and artists, all wear the red and white.

Celebrations follow every trick in the prayer and ritual book. While the priest reads the Catholic Mass – which is broadcast onto the streets outside via loudspeakers for the 100,000 believers that can't fit inside the church – followers of the Afro-Brazilian Umbanda pay homage to Ogum, God of War and equivalent counterpart to Saint George. Through the Catholic Missions, Africans adapted to the new religious concepts by placing holy Catholic figures on their own altars so that they could hold their rituals in the usual manner, but with a nod to Catholicism. So the Umbandistas, officially about two percent of the population of Rio, perform various rituals with the sword of the dragon slayer, often in the shape of a pointed leaf. Sacrifices are made, a glass of beer or sometimes money, and occasionally people fall into a trance when the spirit of Orixá enters their body. And then the priest once more calls over the loudspeakers: "viva São Jorge."

Originally venerated in England, the martyr made his way to Brazil via the Portuguese colonial rulers. In the meantime, several doctoral theses have been written about the Cariocas' deep adoration of him. This saintly symbol of success appears to help establish confidence to surmount the struggles of everyday life.

Address Igreja de São Jorge, corner of Praça da República and Rua da Alfândega 382, Rio de Janeiro, RJ 20061-022 | **Getting there** Metro to Uruguaiana | **Tip** If you can't be in Rio on April 23, the statue of Saint George in the church is impressive even without the procession – or the dragon!

46 __ Feijoada do Salgueiro
Sunday at the samba club

Admission costs around 40 reais, and everyone is welcome. Along with a voucher for food, you will also be handed a T-shirt and a small towel at the door – in case the dancing makes you sweat – all in white and red, the colors of Acadêmicos do Salgueiro Samba School. The hall, and even the furniture, is also decked out in the school's colors. Once a month, the samba school puts on a *feijoada* for everyone, with a whole program of entertainment. There are speeches, sometimes by chairs, sometimes an honorary member says a few words, samba composers present new pieces, or dance groups perform new choreographies. Among the over 100 samba schools in Rio, Salgueiro is one of the oldest and is one of the 12 elite schools that attract many famous composers. They last won the Desfile do Carnaval, or Carnaval Samba Parade, in 2009 and came in a close second in 2015.

The whole event starts off at lunchtime on a Sunday. *Feijoada* is the classic celebration food in Rio. The bean stew with beef and pork is served with *couve a mineira*, a kale dish, *molho de pimenta*, hot chili sauce, and *farofa*, seasoned cassava flour. Gastronomically, the Fejioado do Salgueiro is already on its way to an entry in the gourmet lists of the newspaper *O Globo*, which chooses a winner among 10 samba schools.

The monthly club parties do add something to the samba school's coffers, but most of the money comes from big sponsors, as it takes sums in the millions to make an impression in the parades with brilliance and magnificent costumes. The samba school works the whole year leading up to the Carnaval parade in February, creating concepts, compositions, choreographies, and the parade floats with allegorical representations. Depending on when you visit the club party, you might be lucky enough to see finished choreographies in costume, all in the intimate club atmosphere.

Address Acadêmicos do Salgueiro, Rua Silva Téles 104, Andaraí, Rio de Janeiro, RJ 20541-110, +55 (21) 2238-9226, www.salgueiro.com.br | **Getting there** Metro to Saens Peña, then by foot (around 20 minutes) or taxi | **Hours** See the website for event dates and times. | **Tip** Not far away, the Quadra da Unidos de Vila Isabel Samba School also hosts *feijoada* samba parties. Check their website for dates and information (Boulevard 28 de Setembro 382, Vila Isabel, Rio de Janeiro, RJ 20551-031, www.unidosdevilaisabel.com.br).

47 __ The Fire Station
Emergency call 194

There's a red building on Campo de Santana in the city center that really stands out – it's a work of historicism with striking ornamentation and also Brazil's first fire station. In Brazil, firefighting departments are run by the military and the operational units are made up of full-time soldiers and officers. It follows that every visitor to central command has to show identification and register at the entrance. But there's no sign to indicate a museum is hidden inside.

You enter through the main doors, and once you pass the barrier, you're pretty much inside the first command center of Rio de Janeiro Fire Department, which has remained in operation since 1856. It was right here that the Corpo Provisório de Bombeiros da Corte began its duty, inaugurated by the Portuguese emperor. The pretty building was designed by military engineer Francisco Marcelino de Souza Aguiar later in 1908, with ornamentation using elements from military architecture. The remarkable metal construction in the interior is striking and lends a certain lightness to the whole complex, with apartments, garages for the fire engines, offices, and a canteen.

Don't be surprised if the sirens suddenly call the firefighters into action. They will then rush to their emergency vehicles double-quick, and speed off to the scene of the accident with blue lights flashing. In 2014, the department received the international Conrad Dietrich Magirus award, which recognizes fire departments' exceptional teamwork, for a spectacular operation in the city center after a highway bridge collapsed. They managed to rescue four people from the rubble. A career as a firefighter is highly respected and well paid in Brazil.

In the middle of the fire station there is in fact a small museum, full of historic objects: horse-drawn fire carts, old pumps, old emergency vehicles, as well as historic helmets.

Address Corpo de Bombeiros, Praça da República 45, Centro, Rio de Janeiro, RJ 20211-351, +55 (21) 2333 3133, www.cbmerj.rj.gov.br/museu, contatomuseu@cbmerj.rj.gov.br | **Getting there** Metro to Presidente Vargas | **Hours** Tue–Sat 9am–5pm | **Tip** The 120-piece military orchestra, which used to play every Sunday in the fire station yard, is very well known. Nowadays it occasionally plays on festive occasions.

48__ The Fisherman Colony
Oysters on the beach

The best time to watch the fishermen coming in with their catch is between eight and nine in the morning. It's quiet, the colorful fishing boats land, and the catch is brought ashore in the nets. Posto 6, directly below the fort of Copacabana, is a magical stretch of beach. A bronzed man, Dorival Caymmi, watches on from the sidewalk as the fishermen disentangle, repair, and straighten out their nets. The original creator of bossa nova wrote numerous songs about yearning and the sea, including "Promessa de Pescador" ("The Fisherman's Promise").

The fisherman's association, Colônia dos Pescadores de Copacabana Z13, has existed for over 90 years. Today, it is made up of almost 1,000 fishermen from Urca to Pontal do Recreio and Jacarepaguá, and in Lagoa Rodrigo de Freitas.

Here at Posto 6 there are now around 20 small boats, each with three or four fishermen, who catch fish off the coast in the traditional manner, not from big trawlers. "We set sail every morning between five and half-past and come back at around nine," explains José Manoel Rebouças, Vice-President of the association.

In the past, the Cariocas came directly to the beach to buy huge squid or fish, most of which were fresh and alive. Nowadays much of the catch still lands in the cooking pot that day, but many customers can order by telephone – lobster, tuna fish, or oysters – and everything is delivered to their home. The best restaurants buy their fish and seafood here daily – the oysters come from Florianópolis in the south and are considered the best on the coast.

If you fancy, why not purchase some fresh oysters at the fish shop and enjoy them right here on one of the fishermen's benches? The view of the bay will give you greater appreciation of Dorival Caymmi's music, and maybe there will be some festive fishing boats on their way back to the beach with the catch of the day.

Address Avenida Atlântica, Posto 6, Copacabana, Rio de Janeiro, RJ 22070-002, +55 (21) 2523-4151, www.peixariaz13.com.br | **Getting there** Metro to General Osório, then 15-minutes' walk along Avenida Rainha Elisabeth to the beach | **Hours** Fish shop, daily 8am–2pm | **Tip** Not far off, the legendary Bar Astor, serves a fantastic lychee *caipirinha* (Avenida Vieira Souto 110, Ipanema, Rio de Janeiro, RJ 22420-002, www.barastor.com.br).

49 __ Flaviense Rio Plaza
Where bus drivers stop for a bite

Transvestites, who are regular guests at this bar, always seem to manage to nab one of the six bar stools at the bar. The staff serve them without batting an eyelid; as a rule they order *Coxinha de Frango* (breaded croquettes with a chicken filling) and cola. Both before and after eating they check their make-up carefully in the huge mirror above the only two tables in the joint.

The elderly journalist, who often sits at the back table, looks up briefly from his notes to assure them, with a smile, that they look wonderful.

The bus to Santa Teresa, Rio's Bohemian quarter, stops right in front of the door. Those who take the bus home in the evening, often heavy-laden with bags of shopping, enjoy popping in for a snack or a draught beer and a chat while they wait.

Bus drivers also make use of the chance to go to the toilet, to change money, or to buy a sandwich. Passengers may be forced to wait even longer. Those who complain instantly reveal themselves as outsiders and are punished with unfriendly looks.

Flaviense Rio Plaza is still a real old-school bar in the nightlife-dominated neighborhood of Lapa, and is mainly frequented by regulars. Everything here has been kept simple, nothing has been modernized or made trendy like in many other bars in the area, even if the name suggests otherwise; the words "Flaviense Rio Plaza" are barely legible on the panel above the door. Flaviense is the name of a region in Portugal where the original owners, in the 1950s, came from, but no one really remembers what Rio Plaza refers to, and the *lanconette* is now run by the founder's nephews.

This is a great option any time of day if you want to enjoy some cheap chicken, or anything else fresh from the grill in a truly authentic atmosphere. Or a *pastel* fresh from the oven (pastry with a chicken or cheese filling) or maybe just a cold draught beer (*chope*).

Address Avenida Gomes Frcire 814, corner of Rua Riachuelo, by the bus stop to Santa Teresa, Rio de Janeiro, RJ 20231-015 | **Getting there** Mon–Sat 6pm–1am | **Tip** There's dancing to be had at Lapa 40 Graus, for example the *Gafieira* (partner dance to samba rhythms). (www.lapa40graus.com.br)

50_ The Floating Christmas Tree

Twenty-eight stories of magical lights in the Lagoa

Every year a new spectacle, every year a new theme, every year another choreographer, only the gigantic dimensions stay the same. For almost 20 years, the citizens of Rio de Janeiro have looked forward to a pre-Christmas gift on the first weekend of Advent: the swimming Christmas tree in the Rodrigo de Freitas Lake – the biggest in the whole world.

Eighty-five meters high, 3.1 million light bulbs and 120 kilometers of illuminated ropes on 11 floating carriers – in 2014 it weighed a total of 542 tons. Themes from previous years include, "The Wishes of the Brazilians," "The Wizard of Oz," and "World Peace."

When the lights illuminate the lagoon for the first time on the first Advent Day, up to 200,000 excited people come to watch. Brazilians from all around the country visit the phenomenal Christmas tree, and it already has a place in the *Guinness Book of Records*. After Carnival and New Year's Eve, the inauguration of the Christmas tree is the most important social event in Rio de Janeiro. The opening concert is broadcast live on the Internet. Work on the gigantic structure begins as early as September. Generally standard Christmas lights, just like the ones you wrap around your own tree at home, are used, although it all depends on the design. Around 1,300 people labor over the work of art, from planning to its days of flashing brightly – including building, maintenance, opening ceremony, and deconstruction, all environmentally friendly of course. The huge number of kilowatts that are needed to keep all the lights flashing could provide enough energy for 150 two-bedroom apartments, but at least the electricity is drawn exclusively from sustainable sources.

The Christmas tree is sponsored by the insurance company Bradesco Seguros, which belongs to Banco Bradesco.

Address Visible from many places on the Lagoa Rodrigo de Freitas, Rio de Janeiro, RJ 22470-003 | **Getting there** Metro to General Osório | **Tip** Near Parque da Catacumba, you can take out pedal boats and then pedal around the Christmas tree. Magical!

51 Galeria Novocais

Photography by a delivery driver

The new tram will take you through the middle of Praça Mauá, right down by the sea, and later past decaying factory buildings. Then futuristic skyscrapers suddenly emerge again. Huge shopping centers were to be built here, but so far nothing has happened.

The area around Rio's harbor Porto Maravilha was inaugurated in time for the 2016 Olympic Games, with spectacular new buildings such as the Museu do Amanhã lending it a contemporary look. However, the hopes for the future it inspired failed partly to materialize as the mega event came and went. The permanent exhibition "Porto Cidade – a memória do lugar" has created a place of remembrance for the harbor as it was before the flashy urban development project.

The exhibition illustrates the transformation of the region as it affected the everyday life of the residents in the districts around the harbor with photos, drawings, reproductions, and multimedia tools on 312 square meters of floor space.

Over 600 images from the years 1800 to 1980 were selected from the archives, including the newspapers *O Globo*, and *Jornal do Brasil*, the navy and the National Library. The exhibition in the impressive metal construction (see photo) shows the development of the harbor in chronological order including during its first conversion from 1903 to 1911.

The photographs by Sebastião Pires, a delivery driver from Morro do Pinto, up on the first floor take visitors on an emotional journey into the past. Between 1940 and 1970, Pires documented the locals, the carnival and everyday life, from partying to poverty, in 216 powerful portraits.

The musician and composer Ernesto Nazareth, famous for his *choros* (see ch. 78) and Brazilian tangos, also grew up in the area.

The curators of the exhibition have dedicated three rooms to "the true embodiment of the Brazilian soul," as described by Heitor Villa-Lobos. Here visitors can listen to the great musician's melodies. An emotional and inspiring journey through time.

Address Galeria Novocais, Edifício Novocais, Av. Cidade de Lima 86, Santo Cristo, Rio de Janeiro, RJ, 20220-710 | **Getting there** VLT to Cordeiro da Graça (towards Rodoviária) or Equador (towards Santos Dumont) | **Hours** Mon–Fri 10am–5pm, free admission | **Tip** Nearby, in Samba City (Cidade do Samba) you can enjoy a peak behind the scenes of carnival (with guided tours; information from the tourist office).

52 Galeria Paulo Fernandes

Explosive encounters

You will find *Reclining Venus* (*Vênus Reclinada*), 6 meters long, 1.5 meters high, in a romantic looking corner of the city center. The steel sculpture, created by José Resende, lies in front of Galeria Paulo Fernandes in the middle of the city's "culture corridor," between Casa França-Brasil, Centro Cultural Banco do Brasil, and Centro Cultural dos Correios. While the exhibitions held in the big institutions fill the culture sections of the newspapers, Galeria Paulo Fernandes is all about avant-garde art.

The initial spark for Fernandes' gallery came from the other end of the "culture corridor." In the 1970s, the sculptor, journalist, and alternative filmmaker Jorge O Mourão had his L.O.F.T. Galeria Alternativa here, next to the Carioca aqueduct. His radical Super-8 films still enjoy a cult at festivals, in 2017 a selection was shown at the Tate Gallery in London during "Tropicália and Beyond: Dialogues in Brazilian Film History". His loft was the artistic antithesis to the repressive regime in Brazil during the miilitary dictatorship. Sculptors, theater directors, and musicians met here. "Jorge Mourão is pure avant-garde. He and his Loft have always inspired me. So I searched for a space downtown, even though there were only prostitutes and thieves here at the time." And avant-garde was also what Fernandes presented in 1982, when he opened his gallery with work by the sculptor Nelson Felix. Exhibitions by Tunga, who had become well known in the meantime, Waltércio Caldas, and José Resende, the father of the "Venus," followed. In the meantime, they have all exhibited around the world, including at the documenta, the contemporary art exhibit in Kassel, Germany. In his monumental installation, *In the Light of Two Worlds*, exhibited in the Louvre pyramid in 2005, Tunga showed the mutual relationships between the cultures of the New and Old World. Paulo Fernandes continues to exhibit work by important avant-garde artists in his gallery – a visit is always inspiring.

Address Galeria de Arte Contemporânea Paulo Fernandes, Rua do Rosário 38, on the corner of Rua Visconde de Itaboraí, Centro, Rio de Janeiro, RJ 20041-000, +55 (21) 2233 1537, www.galeriapaulofernandes.com.br | **Getting there** Metro to Uruguaiana | **Tip** Around the corner in Centro Cultural dos Correios, or Post Office Cultural Center (Rua Visconde de Itaboraí 20, Centro, Rio de Janeiro, RJ 20010-060), there are often exciting exhibitions by artists from Rio.

53 Galeto Sat's

Cachaça from a sommelier

Eliane Rabello took over this eatery from her parents, and it has been in the family for over 57 years. They serve fresh, traditional fare here every day, the specialty being *galeto* from a wood-fired grill. The chicken, which mustn't be more than 23 days old, tastes tender and crispy and is very popular among Cariocas. It's especially delicious with the house sauce of orange and hot chili.

In the late evening the place is full, after theater shows and concerts finish and guests come in droves to meet up for a cold beer or a bite to eat.

In the back room of the small, plain bar, a large painting depicts caricatures of big stars such as Maria Bethânia, Zeca Pagodinho, and Chico Buarque, all of whom were once regulars here.

Less well known is the fact that there are about 250 brands of the finest *cachaça* brands on offer here. Eliane and her husband Sergio have been members of the Confraria de Cachaça do Copo Furado (Fraternity of Cachaça of the Leaky Glass) for over 20 years and travel all over Brazil to try out the Brazilian national spirit from practically every single producer. But only companies who produce the sugar cane distillate themselves are taken into consideration – any forms of industrial production are disregarded.

The spirit is tested using strict scientific methods in which the chemical composition is examined carefully. But of course, the flavor is also decisive: "For me, the wood used to mature the cachaça is very important – it makes a huge difference from the very first sniff. But everyone has their own tastes," Eliane explains. She has written about her impressions of every single distillate in her *Book of Wisdom*, which is available for guests to read. It reads a bit like a Gault-Millau wine guide: storage, wooden barrel maturation, flavor, aftertaste, and the like. But most revelers will probably continue to drink their favorite brand.

Address Rua Barata Ribeiro 7, Copacabana, Rio de Janeiro, RJ 22011-001, www.confrariacopofurado.com.br | **Getting there** Metro to Cardeal Arcoverde, then down Rua Barata Ribeiro almost to the end | **Hours** Daily noon–5am | **Tip** Cervantes Restaurant (Rua Barata Ribeiro 7, Copacabana, Rio de Janeiro, RJ 22011-001, www.restaurantecervantes.com.br/lojas) serves delicious sandwiches right into the early hours of the morning.

54 The General's Market
Weekend shopping with samba

The locals call the market the Feira da General, but it is officially the Market on General Glicério Street. This street in the busy, inland neighborhood of Laranjeiras at the feet of the Corcovado is one of the most picturesque, not least because of the ornamented historical houses that line the way. The street is also well known because important samba groups (*blocos*) parade past here during carnival.

The market, which is actually a neighborhood market, takes place every Saturday, featuring fish, vegetables, and fruit, as well as flowers for the Sunday table. The market begins early, and locals often treat themselves to a mid-morning snack of one of the delicious *pastéis* (filled pastries), all of which are homemade and deep fried, with *palmito* (hearts of palm), or with dried meat in the legendary *pastel do bigode* (mustache pastry). Or perhaps a *bolinho de bacalhau* (codfish ball) washed down with *caldo de cana* (sugarcane juice) or coconut water.

The vendors in the square sell arts and crafts as well as all kinds of second-hand goods. If you enjoy a good rummage sale, you're sure to find one or two rare pieces of clothing or costume jewelry. There are even musical instruments to be found. Barraca do Luizinho starts serving *caipirinhas* nice and early.

The musicians assemble at around 11 o'clock in the morning. They are neighbors and friends who play a *choro* (see ch. 78) jam session here after chatting about the events of the week. Many people travel in from other parts of the city to see Pixin-Bodega and Guests. Their name is in honor of Pixinguinha, whose real name was Alfredo da Rocha Viana Filho, and who was the composer responsible for including the saxophone in popular Brazilian music. He wrote approximately 600 *choros*, many of which became classics. Musicians queue up to be the band's "guests." Sometimes they are even students from Europe, who come to learn and add new sounds.

Address Feira da Praça General Glicério, Laranjeiras, Rio de Janeiro, RJ 22245-100, takes place in a street parallel to General Glicério, Rua Professor Ortiz Monteiro, and on the square that it leads onto | **Getting there** Metro to Largo do Machado, then bus 570, 580, 184 etc. to Rua das Laranjeiras próximo ao 515 | **Hours** Sat 8am – 1pm; *choro* from 11am (www.youtube.com/watch?v=U-VYGzcM-Rk) | **Tip** Cantinella Restaurant serves fantastic Italian pasta dishes (Rua General Gliserio 224, Loja D Laranjeiras, Rio de Janeiro, RJ 22245-120, www.massascantinella.com).

55 Gigóia Island

Holidays behind skyscrapers

Barra da Tijuca is the quickest growing neighborhood in Rio, and in the meantime, also one of the more expensive ones. Some call it the Miami of Rio because of all the modern skyscrapers. An eight-lane highway brings busses and cars to the gigantic Barra shopping mall on the Avenida das Américas. It is stressful here, loud and very hectic.

Just next to the shopping mall, though, a narrow path leads off the main road to a jetty. From here, a small motorized boat, a *chalana*, will take you back around 100 years into another world on the little island in the Laguna da Barra da Tijuca within just a few minutes.

People say that it's a bit like the rather rustic northeast of Brazil. There are no cars, no noise, and no rushing around. Some of the streets are not even paved or only secured with large stones. Peace, tranquility, everything about the place is calm. Some Cariocas have little weekend houses here, to which they withdraw in order to take a break from the hustle and bustle of the city now and then.

The island counts 3,000 inhabitants as its own, and they are all awakened in the morning by bird song. In Bar do Galego on Alameda das Mangueiras, Valmir Barbosa has waited every day for over 40 years until the last guest has left. *Allegria sem moderação* (*Fun without moderation*), the bar's motto written on the wall. The sunset here is an unforgettably romantic experience. In fact, everything here is geared towards vacation. The island is very popular on the weekend – in order to offer freshly caught fish in this picturesque surrounding, some restaurants, such as Laguna, are situated right on the water. You can walk the length of Gigóia Island in less than 30 minutes. A total of 11 islands belong to the Laguna Marapendi archipelago, including Ilha dos Pescadores, Fishermen's Island, and Ilha Primeira, which is well known for its fresh seafood.

Address Ilha de Gigóia, Rio de Janeiro, RJ 22641-002 | **Getting there** Bus 181, 301 to Barra Point Shopping (or metro to Jardim when it opens), then follow the path down to the jetty between Unimed and Barra Point to catch a boat to the island | **Tip** You will find wonderful seafood at Bar do Cícero on the neighboring Ilha Primeira (Estrada da Barra 793, Ilha Primeira, Rio de Janeiro, RJ 22641-002, www.bardocicero.com.br).

56 __ The Gilson Martins Shop
The man who plays with Rio

Today he's an internationally renowned artist. Products he designed can be found in museums around the world – you can even buy his bags in the gift shop at the Museum of Modern Art in New York City.

But Gilson comes from very humble beginnings. He spent his childhood in the harbor district, which is now, after its gentrification for the Olympic Games, one of the most upmarket parts of the city, but at the time was one of its poorer areas.

It is this background that inspires Martins' design ideas, all of which play with the classic symbols of Rio: Sugarloaf Mountain, *Christ the Redeemer*, soccer, or the outline of Guanabara Bay.

He began creating bags and accessories by upcycling materials that were discarded, such as fabric remnants, drawer handles, or car seat coverings, and he originally sold them to his fellow students at university. But soon it was the trendy shops that were selling his products, and it wasn't long before Gilson Martins had made a name and a brand for himself.

Today his designs enjoy cult status: backpacks, shopping bags, handbags and purses, iPad protectors, jewelry, and even flip-flops in the bright colors of the Brazilian flag – and all bearing motifs from the "marvellous city" – sell like hotcakes. Gilson opened his first flagship store in 2001 in Ipanema, the Rio district in which Brazil's fashion trends are born. In 2010, he added a shop in Copacabana, and then shortly afterwards another.

Even the Nossa Senhora da Penha Church in the North of the city (see ch. 83), which crowns a hill alongside the notorious Complexo do Alemão favela, became a motif in the designer's work in 2011. And former US First Lady Michelle Obama was given one of his bags when she visited Rio de Janeiro the same year. "Without this city I would never have been where I am now," says Gilson Martins. And he's right.

Address Avenida Atlantica 1998, Rio de Janeiro, RJ 22021-001, +55 (21) 2235-5701, atlantica@gilsonmartins.com.br and Rua Figueiredo Magalhaes 304a, Copacabana, Rio de Janeiro, RJ 22031-010, +55 (21) 3816-0552, copacabana@gilsonmartins.com.br, www.gilsonmartins.com.br | **Getting there** Metro to Siqueira Campos | **Hours** Av. Atlantica: Mon–Sat 9am–9pm, Sun 10am–4pm; Figueiredo Magalhaes: Mon–Fri 9am–8pm, Sat 9am–6pm | **Tip** La Trattoria cooks up delicious Italian pasta (Rua Fernando Mendes 7, Loja A, Copacabana, Rio de Janeiro, RJ 22021-030, www.latrattoriario.com.br).

57_Graffiti Art in Lapa

"Where there's respect, there's peace"

Just a few meters beyond the popular Rua do Lavradio, is the famous Rio Scenarium Bar, a real must-see on the agenda of any serious merrymaker. The bar's size – 335 square meters – and the power of the colors of the mural on the outside wall, on the corner with Rua Visconde do Rio Branco, are impressive from the very first sight. But the story that inspired the artist Panmela Castro to call this mural, *Where There's Respect, There's Peace* (*Onde Há Respeito, Há Paz*) is nothing short of remarkable. Thirteen years ago, Castro was in her early 20s, in love, and just married. But her husband turned out to be abusive, and she ended up fleeing from his beatings.

"Art was the way for me to escape the violence, and I do the same now to continue fighting violence against women," says Castro, alias Anarkia.

The artist and activist is now president of Rede Nami, a non-governmental organization in which 200 women use the medium of art to confront the role of women in Brazilian society, including graffiti workshops and projects at schools that aim to raise awareness and advocate for women's rights.

Anarkia was inspired to paint this mural by children's drawings from one of the organization's projects. It took a full 12 days to complete. It was inaugurated in 2014, on the eighth anniversary of the passing of the Maria da Penha Law, which significantly increased the punishment for those who commit domestic violence against women. The location itself also has a symbolic significance: directly opposite is a police station that specializes in helping women in need, the Delegacia da Mulher, or the Women's Delegation.

The artist is a graduate in painting from the Federal University of Rio de Janeiro and is now well known in Rio's street-art scene. In 2012 she was recognized at the DVF Awards in New York City, which honor brave and strong women.

Address Corner of Rua do Lavradio and Rua Visconde do Rio Branco, Rio de Janeiro, RJ 20230-070, the artist's website: www.panmelacastro.com | **Getting there** Metro to Carioca | **Hours** Unrestricted from the outside | **Tip** Eat great food surrounded by hundreds of pictures of saints at Santo Scenarium (Rua do Lavradio 36, Centro, Rio de Janeiro, RJ 20230-070, www.santoscenarium.com.br), next to the famous Rio Scenarium.

58   Granado Pharmacy
Tropical alchemy

In 1870, Portuguese immigrant José Antônio Coxito Granado founded the Granado Pharmacy on one of the liveliest streets in the city. The store sold products based on plant extracts and flowers with medicinal benefits, which Coxito himself grew in the countryside around Rio de Janeiro. Even today, many Brazilians still trust in the therapeutic effect of plants over pills from the drugstore. Ingredients from Europe, such as sage, are also used.

The quality of the products soon became well known, and it wasn't long until Granado was purveyor to the Emperor's Court. Dom Pedro II also awarded it the title of Official Pharmacy to the Royal Family of Brazil. The recipe for the *polvilho antiséptico* (antiseptic powder) hasn't changed since 1903, and it was one of the first products in Brazil to be patented. Production was soon after relocated to Rua do Senado, where one of the manufacturing facilities is still in operation.

In the 1940s, the Laboratório Chimico-Pharmaceutico Granado was one of the biggest companies in South America and the most renowned in all of Brazil. One of the company's best sellers was a line of glycerin soaps with tropical plant fragrances, which continue in production to this day.

In 1994, after three generations in the family, the Granado Pharmacy was sold to an Englishman, Christopher Freeman, who extended the product range to include cosmetics and perfumes, always in keeping with the tradition and quality of the original plant-based products. The interior of the shop is also befitting and still reminiscent of the era when the emperor would drive by in his carriage. The shampoos, soaps, and creams with tropical plant extracts are still luxury items. Their Castanha do Brasil – Brazil nut shampoos and creams – is well-known for its moisturizing and antioxidant properties, which can be found on offer in swanky hotels and spas.

Address Granado Pharmácias, Rua Primeiro de Março 16, Centro, Rio de Janeiro, RJ 20010-000, www.granado.com.br | **Getting there** VTL tram 2 to Praça XV | **Hours** Mon – Sat 8am – 8pm | **Tip** On Saturdays an antiques and flea market takes place on Praça XV, in front of the pier for the ferry to Niteroi.

59 __ Grumari Beach

Eating crab in paradise!

Every beach in Rio has its own flair: Copacabana is cult, Ipanema fashionable, São Conrado is where the kite-flyers and paragliders land, so it's popular among adventurers, and Prainha is the spot for cool surfers.

On Grumari Beach, you are not really in Rio anymore, but rather on a dream beach in the middle of Bahía, in the land of the blessed. The water of the small, romantic lagoon actually shimmers brownish from the roots of the trees releasing their color into the water. Everything here is natural – the bay is surrounded by hills covered in the trees of the Mata Atlântica, the coastal jungle. The waves break on the beach in high arches, and a fisherman stands on the shore. This is how peaceful it can be here on a weekday.

The Fashion family has been here for 30 years. Raul and Neuza come from the state of Bahía, and much here reminds them of back home. They run the small beach restaurant Rei das Sardinhas, or King of Sardines. Daughter Eliane serves the Cariocas who are after a simple beach idyll far away from the hustle and bustle, especially on the weekend. There are crabs, delivered freshly caught from the other side of the Barra da Guaratiba. They are thrown straight into boiling water, and then you have to figure out how to open them in the traditional fashion, using a little wooden stick to tease out the delicious meat. The *pastel de siri*, fried thin pastry pockets filled with crabmeat, are also delicious. For the slightly different *casquinha de siri*, the crabmeat is removed, cooked, and then served back in the crustacean's own shell. Among the specialties is, of course, *moqueca*, the classic fish stew from Bahía with *dendé* oil and coconut milk. Paradise has nothing on such a feast, as you gaze out to sea with an ice-cold beer in your hand.

At least during the week, that is. On weekends, families with children storm the beach – and everyone is in the best of spirits.

Address Rei das Sardinhas, Praia do Grumari, Avenida Estado da Guanabara, Recreio dos Bandeirantes, Rio de Janeiro, RJ 22785-250 | **Getting there** Metro L1, L4 to Jardim Oceanico, then bus 2334 or 2335 to Ricreio dos Bandeirates, then taxi, there is no public transport to this beach | **Hours** Daily 8am–6pm | **Tip** Praia do Abricó, around 3.5 kilometers to the east, is the only nudist beach in Rio (Grumari, Rio de Janeiro, RJ, www.anabrico.com).

60 Guaratiba Rock

At the Mother of God's favorite place

In the past Pedra de Guaratiba, or Garatiba Rock, on the coast around 60 kilometers south of the city center, was the place from which gold from Minas Gerais was exported around the world. Today, Cariocas from other neighborhoods like to come to the small fishing village, especially to enjoy beautifully prepared fresh fish in laid-back surroundings.

Walking on the pier at sunset is simply beautiful. Herons sit calmly on the jetty that leads out into the Atlantic Ocean. It is peaceful and idyllic here. On the coast towards the East, just separated from the sea by the road, is a small and rather surprising church that deserves your attention. The fourth oldest Catholic church in Rio de Janeiro, Nossa Senhora do Desterro, dates from the year 1628 and is a real gem. The unusual façade is almost completely covered in tiles, and this house of worship has been landmarked since 1938.

And it also stands on an enchanting square. According to legend, an old Native American woman worked for Jerônimo and his wife Beatriz. The servant was blind and sick. One day she came to her masters with a request: the Mother of God had appeared to her in a dream and had said that the masters should build a house of God by the sea in her honor. At first, the couple was suspicious and did not believe her. But one morning, the woman woke and was neither sick nor blind. On the contrary, she was, miraculously, young and beautiful. The couple went straight to work looking for the perfect location, and they chose this romantic place for the church. The Carmelites wanted to relocate the church and rebuild it in front of their convent, but they found any work done during the day had been razed to the ground by the next morning.

True or not, this place is really enchanting. Opposite the church, you can order a cold beer in a small shack under a shady tree and look out across the sea.

Address Igreja Nossa Senhora do Desterro, Rua Barros de Alarcão, Pedra de Guaratiba, Rio de Janeiro, RJ 23027-340 | **Getting there** Train from Central to Santa Cruz, or at the other end of the route Castelo, then bus (Frescão) 2381 or 2335 to Pedra da Guaratiba (50 minutes to one and a half hours depending on traffic) | **Tip** The *langoustines a malandrinho* in the restaurant Amendoeira, are unbeatable (Rua Barros de Alarcão 1015, Pedra de Guaratiba, Rio de Janeiro, RJ 23027-340, www.restauranteamendoeira.com.br).

61 The Hanging Gardens
A touch of Parisian flair

A set of stairs leads up from the harbor to the hanging gardens of Valongo. Rio's harbor itself was once called Cais do Valongo, or Valongo Wharf when around 500,000 slaves arrived here between 1769 and 1830. Despite their history, this enchanting landscape architecture was the result of urban development measures undertaken in 1906.

The romantic gardens with their small pathways were meant to serve the members of "refined society" for their afternoon strolls. They were once decorated with statues of Roman deities made of real Carrara marble. Under mayor Francisco Pereira Passos, the then capital of Brazil experienced the biggest visible change in its history: dilapidated colonial structures were torn down, and many buidlings were bulldozed in order to make space for grand boulevards with modern buildings, such as the Avenida Rio Branco. The idea was that Rio de Janeiro should become a "Paris of the Tropics." Stately buildings from this period include the Municipal Theater, the National Museum of Fine Arts, and the National Library.

The gardens of Valongo were over 1,500 square meters in size at the time and originally served in supporting the hillside of Morro da Conceição. "Fattening houses" – shacks in which slaves were forced to gain weight in order to increase their price at market – once stood here.

The design of the gardens came from the pen of landscape architect Luis Rey and is inspired by the French parks of the 19th century. There were terraces with pathways, trees, green areas and flowers, a vegetable garden, and a toolshed. Unfortunately, the gardens were neglected for several decades and were even misused as a garbage dump. The gardens were finally renovated in the course of the work to renew the area around the harbor, Porto Maravilha, and are now once again an oasis of peace. Occasionally they even provide a poetic setting for photo shoots.

Address Jardim Suspenso do Valongo, Rua Camerino at the level of Preço dos escravos, Rio de Janeiro, RJ 20080-010 | **Getting there** Metro to Presidente Vargas or Uruguaiana | **Hours** Unrestricted | **Tip** There is a lively outdoor samba session every Friday evening on the small plaza nearby, Pedra do Sal, on the edge of the harbor area (R. Argemiro Bulcão, s/n, Saúde, Rio de Janeiro, RJ 20081-040).

62 __ The Horto Waterfall

Rainforest shower

Rio de Janeiro is the only city in the world that has a municipal rainforest. The Tijuca National Park is an oasis in the middle of the urban jungle, a piece of Atlantic Rainforest, but *de facto* a different entity all its own: the park is the work of a gigantic reforestation effort in 1861 on the orders of Emperor Dom Pedro II.

The actual rainforest fell victim to coffee cultivation. Through the felling of the trees that had protected the springs, the water supply began to dry up, and the region was well on its way to degenerating into a desert.

In the hour of need, the emperor ordered the land's expropriation and reforestation. Today, there are snakes, iguanas, ocelots, sloths, and howler monkeys living here. The nature park stretches over 100 square kilometers and is definitely worth an exploratory tour.

On particularly hot days, when the beaches are bustling with activity, many locals seek refreshment in the cool rainforest. From one of the entrances to the Tijuca Forest, near the Municipal Botanical Gardens, you can also access the Horto waterfall. The path up to it takes, depending on your condition, around 20 minutes. It is shady and cool, and intertwining forest paths lead upwards; tree roots serve as stairs, and at two or three places you have to climb a little, but children can manage it too. The waterfall is popular among families, especially on the weekend. It is glorious to let the ice-cold water, which flows through the rocks in the cave, clatter onto your shoulders – you'll feel like you're in a lovely, cooling shower. Or sit in the natural swimming pool and just relax.

Many come to the waterfall at the beginning of the year, in order to start the New Year – after bathing in the sea on New Year's Eve – with a shower under the waterfall. "It cleanses the soul and gives you positive energy," is the general sentiment.

Address Cascada do Horto, Floresta da Tijuca, entrance Rua Pacheco Leão, Jardim Botânico, Rio de Janeiro, RJ 22460-030 | **Getting there** Bus 409 Saens Peña – Jardim Botânico, to Horto (Rua Othon Bezerra de Melo), then by foot into Rua Pacheco Leão and then on to the Horto turn off | **Tip** A guided tour through the rainforest is exciting. Book at www.rionatural.com.br.

63 — The Jesuit Bridge
Brilliant hydraulic engineering of the 18th century

The neighborhood of Santa Cruz, now a residential area 60 kilometers from the city center, experienced an economic boom during the 17th and 18th centuries with new irrigation technology at the Fazenda de Santa Cruz.

The whole area was gifted as a reward to Cristovão Monteiro, comrade-in-arms of the Chief Officer Estácio de Sá during the ejection of the French from Rio de Janeiro in 1567. He founded a *fazenda*, or farming estate, which was bequeathed to the Jesuit Society of Jesus by his widow 20 years later. The society organized the Native American missions into small *aldeias*, or working communities, which were similar to the collectives of the former Soviet Union, and also introduced a Christian social system. Recognized by the crown, the Jesuits thus had an institutional status that greatly exceeded the religious character of their order.

In this way the Jesuit *fazenda* rapidly developed into a profitable endeavor. The padres bred livestock and produced a variety of agricultural products. However, they also had 430 enslaved families working for them, according to inventory documents.

In order to connect the *fazenda* with the city, the Jesuits beat a road right through the fields and built a bridge. Padre Pero Fernandes was the architect of the structure, built in 1752. It also had the added function of regulating the flow of water irrigating the rice fields but never flooding them. The bridge served as a sluice, with four arches of different sizes, so that the water would drain off when levels were high or could be dammed if needed. Of course, it was also the pedestrian crossing for travelers who were on their way from the interior of the country to the coast.

This hydraulic engineering feat from colonial Brazil – 50 meters long and 6 meters wide – was recently restored and can be found in the middle of some fields close to a small farm.

Address Ponte dos Jesuítas, Estrada do Cortume next to the Ponte Lindolfo Color, Rio de Janeiro, RJ 23560-130 | **Getting there** Train to Santa Cruz, then bus or van to Ponte dos Jesuítas | **Hours** Unrestricted | **Tip** The former Fazenda dos Jesuítas on Avenida do Matadouro, which became the Antiga Fazenda Imperial de Santa Cruz after the expulsion of the Jesuits, is worth a small detour.

64 Klussmann Square

The Jungle Book by a math teacher

All the math teacher really wanted to do was make something nice for his children – a magical world of animals. Paulo de Tarso ended up creating almost 100 concrete sculptures, a menagerie of animals and mythical figures from Brazil's famous children's books.

This quirky yet idyllic little corner of the neighborhood of Tijuca is in the middle of a magical little forest, almost in Alto da Boa Vista. The open-air museum is actually still a playground. At least that's how the parents in the area see it – it is another popular place to host birthday parties.

It is in part the childlike fantasy that makes this place special in its own way. But it is also the place itself, an enchanting piece of original Tijuca Forest that leads to Rio Trapicheiros – it could be the setting for a Brazilian *Jungle Book*. As an artist, Paulo de Tarso approached his sculptures through the eyes of a child. Each individual figure suggests its own world of experience, not so unlike the video games of today. The camel, for example, seems to conjure up the heat of the desert.

Drawing on Brazilian children's literature, Paulo de Tarso created Emília, the talking doll from the work of the most famous Brazilian children's author Monteiro Lobato. She resembles Pippi Longstocking, Popeye, Felix the Cat, and Peter Pan, all of whom inspired Monteiro Lobato's writing. A polar bear has certainly made his home here in the fairytale forest; a chieftain dwells at the far side; a pink elephant, who looks like Dumbo, sits close by – and don't miss the ostrich.

Letting yourself be carried off into a world of childlike fantasy is a particularly good way to enjoy the almost surreal atmosphere here, right next to the actual jungle. Look for a little detour at the end of the picturesque street in the middle of this middle-class residential area of Tijuca that leads to a waterfall. Enchanting!

Address Praça Hans Klussmann, Rua Sabóia Lima, Tijuca, Rio de Janeiro, RJ 20521-250 |
Getting there Metro to Uruguaiana, then by foot along Rua Conde de Bonfim, turn right
into Rua José Higino to Praça Gabriel Soares, cross the square and then a half right into
Rua Sabóia Lima to Praça Klussmann at Parque Florestal da Tijuca | **Tip** Cantina da Nonna
serves *galetos*, delicious, pizza-like flatbreads, in the evening (Rua Conde de Bonfim 601,
Tijuca, Rio de Janeiro, RJ 20520-052).

65 — The Legalize Drinks Stand

Sharing a Madame Satã

Before the curtains part in *Circo Voador*, or Flying Circus, one of the most fashionable stages in the city, many theater goers stop in front of the door for a drink against the nighttime backdrop of the radiant white arches of the Arcos da Lapa aqueduct, which runs right through the middle of the city.

Among the many stalls that offer drinks and snacks, Legalize Drinks rises above: Juares used to be a barman in the biggest hotels in Rio. He knows his stuff and mixes both classics and his own creations. The *Madame Satã*, for example, with cachaça, lime, mint, ginger, and sugar, is an homage to the real Madame Satan, who was legendary in Arcos da Lapa from the 1920s through the 1950s, at the time when the area was defined by prostitution and petty criminality. A homosexual and transvestite, who regularly landed in prison, he later became a celebrity. The Brazilian-Algerian film director and visual artist Karim Aïnouz brought the story of Madam Satan to the big screen, and it premiered at Cannes International Film Festival in 2002.

Or try a *Negrito* – with chocolate, condensed milk, mint, and ice – another creation, which Juares' partner Tania dedicated to her sweetheart. When the former primary school teacher and the barkeeper first met, they only had a polystyrene box full of cold drinks, which they would offer to festival-goers – they followed the big shows right through the city – until one day a tourist couple from Australia – impressed by the delicious drinks and the friendly pair of lovers – bought them a bicycle with a trailer. This was a quantum leap – trips through the city with all of those bottles were hard work.

For several years now, the two of them have had a permanent stand at Arcos da Lapa and have made a name for themselves with their *Caipi-Fruttas* with vodka, strawberries, passion fruit, pineapple, or cashew and condensed milk.

Address Legalize Drinks, Arcos da Lapa, Rio de Janeiro, RJ 20230-06, right in front of the entrance to Circo Voador | **Getting there** Metro to Cinelândia, then walk along Rua Evaristo da Veiga to the square with the aqueduct | **Hours** Thu – Sat 7pm – 4am | **Tip** Churrasco do Branco serves delicious little kebabs (*churrasco*), in front of the building that used to house legendary artists' lofts (see ch. 52) in Lapa.

66 Luiz' Fish Stand

On the beach of lovers

This place is only ever really busy on Sundays. Families with children, armed with buckets and spades, ready for a perfect day on the beach, can hardly contain their excitement on the one-and-a-half-hour ferry ride across Guanabara Bay to Paquetá Island. Paquetá, only eight kilometers in circumference, is a neighborhood of Rio, except here everything is peaceful and above all – safe.

Way back in 1555, Paquetá Island was settled by the French, but it soon fell into Portuguese hands. At the beginning of the 19th century Dom João VI, King of Portugal, discovered the picturesque beaches and romantic walking trails.

Bohemians hung out here in the 1950s – the first naked woman on the beach caused a huge scandal. Nowadays, on public holidays, a regular stream of day-trippers flows from the jetty to the family beach, where pink or bright green pedal boats and huge swan boats can be rented out. A little further on, however, it is a lot more peaceful. The Pedra dos Namorados (Lovers' Stone) is pretty much the Trevi Fountain of Paquetá in the form of a huge stone on the beach: if the pebble you toss in doesn't fall off the stone, then it must be love!

Praia da Moreninha is the most beautiful beach on the island.

Luiz' family has been serving freshly caught fish here, on little wobbly tables under a parasol, for 40 years. His wife Conceição says that her father always sold fresh fish here too. Up until a few years ago, they would also fry the fish on a barbecue on the spot on weekends. But the municipal authorities banned this menu item on hygiene grounds. So now, Conceição takes the order, and Luiz fries the fish at home, just 100 meters away. The teamwork is as quick as a flash, and the table is laid in no time too. *Tainha* (mullet) is the name of the fish caught directly in the bay, and it tastes simply delicious fried.

Address Praia da Moreninha, Ilha de Paquetá, Rio de Janeiro, RJ 20397-250, near Pedra dos Namorados | Getting there Ferry to Ilha de Paquetá from the ferry terminal on Praça XV, around 70 minutes journey time, 5am–11pm, roughly every three hours, www.barcas-sa.com.br | Tip On the right side of the beach there's a kind of secret passage through the rocks to Praia de São Roque, where it's peaceful even on holidays.

67 Madureira Hyper Market

Chickens for the gods

During the train journey, you experience the charms of the Rio's periphery: traveling salesmen peddling headphones and other electronic equipment, peanut vendors, and occasionally musicians. Fellow passengers are a mixed bag, ranging from office suits to laborers in *havaianas*, or rubber flip-flops. The destination is Madureira in the north of Rio. Once you arrive, you first have to cross a viaduct, zigzagging to get to the other side of the highway. The atmosphere here already begins to simmer, and there's something for sale every few steps: Mickey Mouse T-shirts, candy, drinks, and coconuts.

The Mercadão Madureira is the equivalent of a "hypermarket": 580 shops attract over 100,000 people from Rio and the surrounding region every day. When the market was founded in 1914, there was only food. The hall was restored after a fire and now presents itself proudly with elevators, air conditioning, and security guards.

A walk around reveals many colors, aromas, and surprising encounters. Goods range from nail polish in 3,000 colors and costume jewelry, to everything you need to build a kite. The smell of aromatic and medicinal herbs will greet you on the second floor. On the stall run by Célia, who is now over 90 years old, there is *abajerú* to combat high cholesterol levels and *sete-sangrias* for high blood pressure. *O astral* helps to improve your aura, and *macaçá* is the herb that calls out to love … dried codfish, candied fruit, drinks from sparkling wine to imported whiskey, wedding dresses, kitchen utensils, Minnie Mouse and Snow White costumes.

There are 25 shops dedicated to the spiritual life and life-sized statues of saints. In O Mundo dos Orixás (World of the Spirits), you can find citronella for friendship and herbs for cleansing the soul. Chickens and doves are sold on the first floor – not for your dinner, but for use in ritual sacrifices.

Address Mercadão de Madureira, Avenida Ministro Edgard Romero 239, Madureira, Rio de Janeiro, RJ 21360-901, www.mercadaodemadureira.com | **Getting there** Supervia train from Central to Madureira, check here for the train schedule: www.supervia.com.br; *carioca* Ivo Korytowski offers English language tours in the neighborhood of Madureira (ivikory@gmail.com) | **Hours** Mon–Sat 7am–7pm, Sun & holidays 7am–noon | **Tip** Once a year in the nearby Oswaldo Cruz neighborhood is a big samba party (Trem do Samba). See website for dates and details (www.tremdosambaoficial.com.br).

68__Madureira Viaduct
The charm of Baile Charme

The atmosphere under the steel girders that support the viaduct over the multilane highway comes to a boil from midnight every Saturday. Hot rhythms and the sound of the hippest DJs, who have been making music here for over 20 years, are the hallmarks of *Baile Charme*, or the Charm Dance. The event began in the 1990s in the *favelas* in the northern part of the city, which were shaken by gangs and drug wars at the time. In the meantime, the Saturday evening dance event has been declared a cultural asset.

At the time, when a group of street vendors were looking to promote it, *música charme* was still relatively unknown. The expression was first coined for a variety of R&B created by DJ Corello back to the early 1980s. In the beginning, the initiators Celso Athayde and his brother Cesar borrowed the sound equipment from a friend, the funk expert DJ Marlboro. Back then the ground it stood on wasn't even flat. Their mother lent the brothers money so they could purchase drinks to sell – there were no other sources of income.

Famous DJs, including American Keith Sweat, one of the biggest names in R&B, helped make the event famous. The success of the telenovela *Avenida Brasil* in 2012, in which the viaduct played a main role, was partly responsible for the diversity of the audience. To that point, it had been almost exclusively made up of people from the outskirts in the North of the city, but now dance lovers from Copacabana and Ipanema on the southern beaches also come to join in the fun.

The *baile* is very emotional. Dancers follow choreographed sequences by the *charmeiros do viaduto*, the viaduct charmers, who have even been awarded the Halley Prize for their achievements. Some of them have gone on to become well-known choreographers. DJ Michell, who has been part of it all since the beginning, invites anyone who would like to experience the *baile* to come along: "Everyone here is in party mood and peaceful."

Address Baile Charme, Viaduto Negrão de Lima, Madureira, Rio de Janeiro, RJ 21350-180, www.viadutodemadureira.com.br, contato@viadutodemadureira.com.br | **Getting there** Train from Central to Madureira, way back only by taxi | **Hours** Sat from 10pm (if the weather is fine) | **Tip** Nearby at Papa G. (Tv. Almerinda Freitas 42, Madureira, Rio de Janeiro, RJ 21350-280), you can find cool cocktails and passionate music at the weekend from 11pm.

69 __ The Magdalena Chapel

Baroque dream

Roberto de Regina is 90 years old and has dedicated his whole life to baroque music. He was responsible for the building of the first *cembalos*, or harpsichords, in Brazil and founded the famous Camerata Antiqua of Curitiba.

By 1991, he had had enough of concert tours and withdrew to this secluded place: a magical park with a pond, through which a dozen peacocks strut, proudly displaying their tail feathers, and a stately home. In order to continue celebrating early music, he decided to set up one of the rooms as a chapel. It took many years until it was completed. De Regina didn't always stick to the Bible for the motifs, and one or two of the figures are quite surprising, such as the one of Atlas, who was actually supposed to hold up the roof but has abandoned his position, enraptured by the baroque sounds no doubt – a little joke on de Regina's account. The heads of great Baroque musicians adorn the ceiling, and the atmosphere reflects the music.

De Regina regularly organizes concerts here, which include dinner or lunch. Everything has to be just right: the reception in historical garments in the park, the light in the chapel, the dishes. The whole event feels like a journey back in time! Roberto de Regina wants his guests to experience the music intensely. In the Ronaldo Ribeiro Museum next door, de Regina presents his personal journey across the globe. Cathedrals from around the world, from Notre-Dame to Cologne, are exhibited in miniature form, all built by de Regina himself. "At some point, I had made so many things that I didn't know what to do with them." And thus the museum was born. In the "transport" section, he has cut a model of a Zeppelin right through the middle and reproduced the interior design by hand, revealing the architect in him.

A trip to the Magdalena Chapel grants a small insight into the world of this illustrious artist – and you're sure to leave enchanted by its many facets and charms.

Address Estrada do Mato Alto 6024, Barra de Guaratiba, Rio de Janeiro, RJ 23020-700, +55 (21) 2410-7183 / 988-515-052, www.capelamagdalena.com.br. Reservations at contato_capelamagdalena@yahoo.com.br, also in English | **Getting there** Express bus BRT Mato Alto, www.brtrio.com/estacoes (transport in a minibus is included when booking a concert ticket, pick up at hotel) | **Hours** Variable. Contact the chapel for information and reservations. | **Tip** Only eight kilometers away, you can eat excellent fish in the idyllic ambiance of the Tia Palmira Restaurant (Caminho do Souza 18, Barra de Guaratiba, Rio de Janeiro, RJ 23020-240).

70 __ Manequinho
The peeing mascot

A survey of the fans of Botafogo Soccer Club asking why a little peeing boy is their club's mascot resulted in a wide variety of responses. "Because he pisses on anyone who deserves it." "Because every man has peed on the street at some point." "Because he represents the young players from back then when the club was successful." The truth, however, is very different.

The statue, which is quite reminiscent of the *Manneken Pis* in Brussels, Belgium, was first installed on the Floriano Peixoto Plaza in the city center in 1914. Created by Sculptor Belmiro de Almeida, the piece was actually inspired by the stubborn character of politician Rivadávia Correia. The statue's most striking commonality with its Belgian brother is the fact that they are both urinating. Otherwise, Manequinho differs in many details, particularly in size: Manequinho is 1 meter, or 3¼ feet tall, compared to Manneken Pis at just 61 centimeters, or two feet.

In 1919, Mayor Paulo de Frontin unceremoniously ordered that the statue be removed, and it was placed in a warehouse. The protests of the press and art lovers didn't change the mayor's mind. But in 1927 the peeing boy was installed once again – this time in Botafogo, in front of the soccer club's offices.

In 1957, the club won the city championships, an ecstatic fan dressed the little man in his sweaty jersey – and so he became the unofficial club mascot. It wasn't until 1991 that Manequinho officially replaced Donald Duck as their lucky charm, when Walt Disney began demanding license fees.

To this day, the little peeing boy is dressed in a club jersey every time his team wins a title. The lad has been through quite a lot. He was stolen in 1990 and replaced with a replica in 1993 upon the insistence of the general public. In 2008 his penis was stolen, but fortunately for everyone it was later recovered and resecured.

Address Botafogo de Futebol e Regatas, Avenida Venceslau Brás 72, Botafogo, Rio de Janeiro, RJ 21853-480 | **Getting there** Metro to Botafogo, then bus 104, 426, etc. to Góis Monteiro próximo ao 146 | **Tip** The building that houses Botafogo Football Club stands out from the urban landscape through its striking historicist architecture.

71 Maria and Getúlio's

Stew in two-four time

Looking at the huge building that houses the Nordestinos Market from the outside, you get a feeling for how many of Rio de Janeiro's current residents came to the city from the northeast of the country to look for happiness and opportunity here. In the meantime, they are a fixed part of Rio's population – and this market is where they keep the traditions of their home alive.

Products from the northeast – cassava roots, Malagueta pepper, tapioca flour, handicrafts – are on sale in the market's 700 stalls. Musical groups play dance music from the region, from *Forró* to *Xote* in two-four time, on several stages every evening from Thursday to Saturday. Then – to put it mildly – all hell breaks loose here until four in the morning.

Maria's parents also come from the northeast of the country, from the small city of Piani. Maria's father immigrated to Rio to find work. After working several odd jobs, he decided he would open a stall. That was 33 years ago. Back then, the immigrants peddled their goods in the open air, as the huge hall didn't exist yet. Together with his wife, he prepared hearty specialties from the Old Country with their typical spices. *Rabada* (braised oxtail) for example, or *sarapatel* (pigs' or sheep's liver and heart cooked in blood with tomatoes, chili pepper, and onions). There is also *baião de dois*: rice, mixed with baked beans and cheese, often with cassava or potato chips; or *carne de sol*: thin strips of beef that have been salted and laid out to dry in the sun for two to four days.

All of these dishes are still available today, though Tatjana, Getúlio and Maria's daughter, has taken over the helm in the meantime. She no longer serves her dishes from a ramshackle construction trailer, but rather at smart wooden tables. The restaurant is located right next to the big stage, and dancing is most definitely allowed on the weekend!

Address Maria and Getúlio Altura, Fiera de São Cristóvão 260, Centro Cultural Luiz Gonzaga, Campo de São Cristóvão, São Cristóvão, Rio de Janeiro, RJ 20921-440, www.mariaegetulio.com.br, +55 (21) 2589-5890 | **Getting there** Metro to São Cristóvão, then around 20-minutes' walk or bus 313, 327, etc. to Campo São Cristóvão próximo ao 369 | **Hours** Tue–Thu 11am–4pm, Fri & Sat 10–4am, Sun 5–9pm | **Tip** On weekends there is also traditional live music on the small stage.

72 Mayrink Chapel
Mass under the lianas

Mayrink Chapel is a real surprise in the middle of the Tijuca Forest, with its candy-pink exterior. Famous singers and stars come here to say, "I do." It's certainly very romantic here in the middle of the rainforest. And historic. Inside the chapel, there are replicas of work by Candido Portinari (1903 – 1962) to be admired, including *Nossa Senhora do Carmo*, *São João da Cruz*, *São Simão Stock* and *Purgatório*. Acclaimed landscape architect Roberto Burle Marx designed the garden around the chapel. The two statues at the entrance are from a church on Avenida Presidente Vargas that no longer exists.

This chapel was built in 1850 by Count Antonio Alves Souto and then sold to Baron von Mesquita, who declared Nossa Senhora do Carmo as its patron saint. The color pink is original and was popular among the powerful coffee barons at the time – the color stands for the family. Later, the chapel was sold to Francisco de Paula Mayrink, whose name it has borne to this day.

Initially, four originals by Candido Portinari were at home here. Born the son of Italian immigrants on a coffee plantation in the state of São Paulo, Portinari studied modern South American painting at the Escola Nacional de Belas Artes, or the National School of Fine Arts. He spent time in Europe from 1928 to 1930, and upon his return, he turned to a socially critical, expressive painting style, influenced by Muralismo. His most significant work includes wall paintings, including *War and Peace* in the United Nations Headquarters in New York City, and *Primeira Missa no Brasil* (*The First Mass in Brazil*), which remains in Brazil.

The original works at the chapel were stolen, but later reappeared. They were then given a safe home in the Museu Nacional de Belas Artes. The replicas in the church are very impressive nonetheless. Mass is held at 12:30pm on the first Sunday of every month – a truly unique experience.

Address Estrada da Cascatinha 850, Alto da Boa Vista, Rio de Janeiro, RJ 20531-590 | **Getting there** Metro to Saens Peña, then taxi or bus 301 or 345 to the entrance to Parque Nacional da Tijuca, then follow signage to Cascatinha Taunay | **Hours** Daily 2–4pm, Mass is given monthly on the first Sunday at 12:30pm | **Tip** The Taunay Waterfall is on the same path and is the largest waterfall in the Tijuca Park.

73 _ The Mesbla Lighthouse
Clock with an element of nostalgia

What is a clock doing at the top of a lighthouse? The lighthouse itself is run by the Port Authorities, and it is there to signal ships making their way through Guanabara Bay when they approach Paquetá Island.

But the clock on it comes from the department store company Mesbla, which was one of the leading companies in the country right up into the 1990s, with 180 branches nationwide. The most profitable period in the company's history was during the 1980s, when you could even purchase a brand new car with a Mesbla credit card, truly unheard of at the time. In 1999, however, the company fell on hard times and filed for bankruptcy, unable to keep pace with the rapid changes in the market.

Mesbla first opened in 1924 with a single department store in Rio de Janeiro on Passeio Público. The building was crowned by a huge clock on its spire, which told the time with Swiss precision, not something to be taken for granted in an age when the digital clock had not yet been invented.

An identical model of the huge clock can still be admired to this day, adorning the Paquetá lighthouse, as the Colônia de Férias da Mesbla, the Mesbla Vacation Colony, was located just opposite the site. The managing directors set great store in their employees' well-being and the employees were proud of their company. At the start of the 1960s, when ferries like the Vital Brazil or Boa Viagem were constantly crossing the bay from Niterói with 2,000 passengers at a time, the company suggested the coastguard should erect a lighthouse. The rectangular cement tower, 9.45 meters, or 31 feet tall, also has a siren. The ceremonial inauguration of the lighthouse took place in August 1966, in the presence of high-ranking naval officers. The distinctive signal is visible from far and wide and is located in a particularly idyllic area of Paquetá Island that is terribly romantic around sunset.

Address Praia das Gaivotas, Rio de Janeiro, RJ 20396-060 | **Getting there** Ferry to Ilha de Paquetá from the downtown ferry terminal Praça XV, around 70 minutes, weekdays 5am–11pm, around every three hours, www.barcas-sa.com.br | **Hours** Unrestricted from the outside | **Tip** If you would like to extend your stay: Hospedaria Ilha de Paqueta (Rua Tomás 151, Paqueta, CEP 20397-125), for reservations contact Alexadre +55 (21) 97246-6585 or use booking.com.

74 The Monument to Zumbi
The beheaded

On the multilane Avenida Presidente Vargas is a monument dedicated to the "black leader of all races," Zumbi dos Palmares (1655 – 1695), who successfully resisted the colonial government in the north of Brazil. The spot itself is not particularly remarkable, although its proximity to Praça Onze, which is known as the cradle of samba and Afro-Brazilian culture in Rio, is important. Nevertheless, the monument draws attention, not least because of its size.

The concrete and metal sculpture was inaugurated in 1986 as the largest symbol and monument to the Negritude Movement, the international reclamation of the African identity. Darcy Ribeiro (1922 – 1997), an ethnologist, intellectual, and vice-minister for culture at the time, was one of the initiators in the creation of this monument. Ribeiro commissioned the architect João Filgueiras Lima to depict the martyr, and he came up with a design for a monument over seven meters high.

The concrete pyramid is clad with marble, and a bronze head weighing 800 kilograms is fixed to the top. This was, in fact, the way the life of Zumbi dos Palmares ended on November 20, 1695. After being decapitated, his head was displayed in public in order to convince the African slaves that he was dead – to this point they had thought he was immortal.

The head is based on a sculpture of a preexistent likeness from the 17th century, which is an exhibit in the British Museum in London as an eternal symbol for the *beleza negra*, the beauty of black culture. Dia da Consciência Negra (Black Consciousness Day) is commemorated annually at the hero's memorial on November 20. Representatives of the syncretic religions Candomblé and Umbanda celebrate together with folkloristic carnival groups such as the Filhos de Gandhi or dance to music by Gilberto Gil. On this day, at least, the place is filled with joy and gladness.

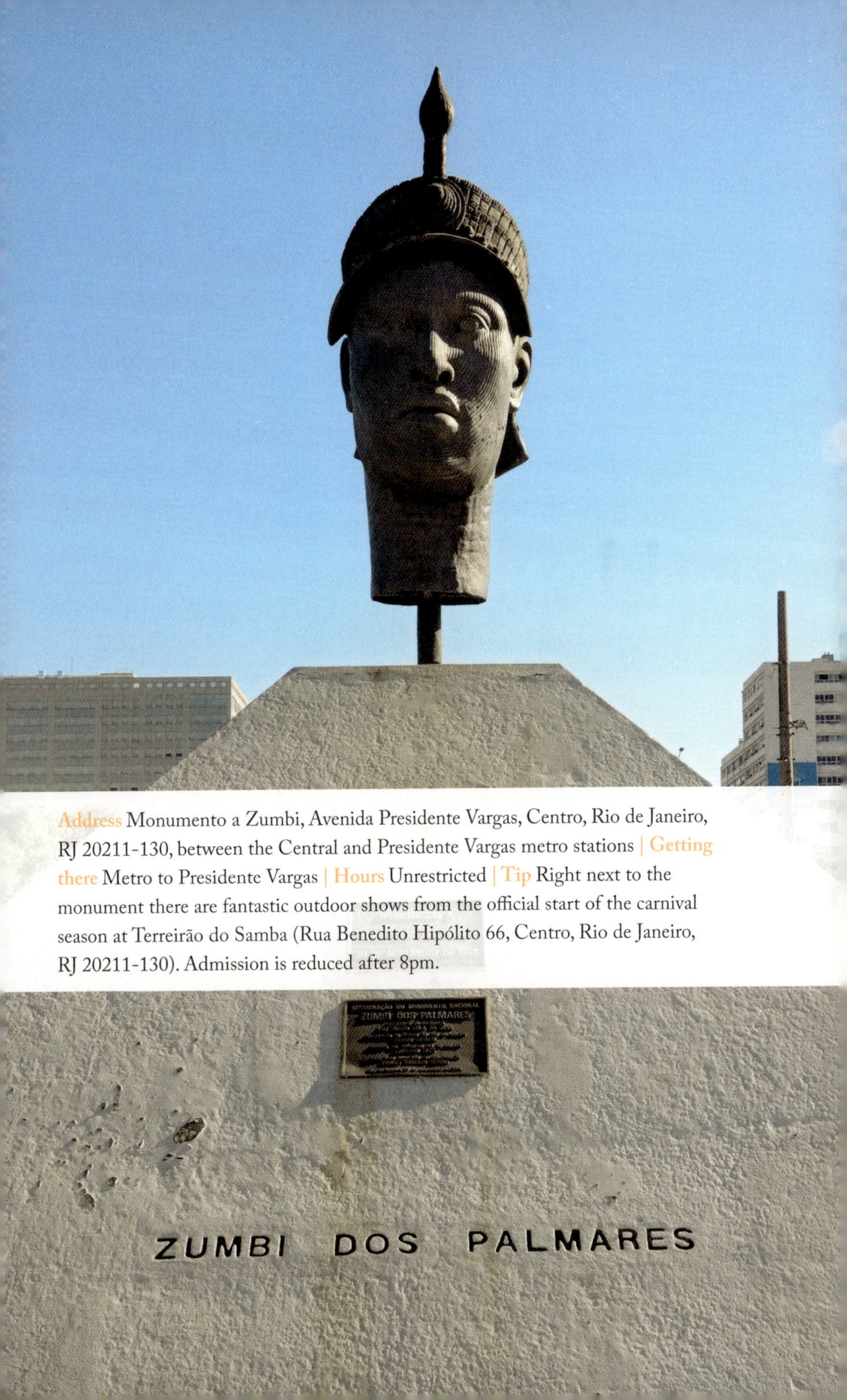

Address Monumento a Zumbi, Avenida Presidente Vargas, Centro, Rio de Janeiro, RJ 20211-130, between the Central and Presidente Vargas metro stations | **Getting there** Metro to Presidente Vargas | **Hours** Unrestricted | **Tip** Right next to the monument there are fantastic outdoor shows from the official start of the carnival season at Terreirão do Samba (Rua Benedito Hipólito 66, Centro, Rio de Janeiro, RJ 20211-130). Admission is reduced after 8pm.

ZUMBI DOS PALMARES

75__ The Moreira Salles House
The magic of Burle Marx

The son of the art-loving Moreira Salles family, Walter Salles, is considered one of the best feature-film directors in the world. His film *Central Station* received the Golden Bear at the Berlinale in 1998 and a Golden Globe in 1999, and his 2004 movie *The Motorcycle Diaries*, a story based on the personal writings of Ernesto "Che" Guevara, quickly became a box-office hit around the world.

The director's father Walter Moreira Salles (1912–2001), a private banker and former ambassador in the United States in the 1950s, was dedicated to art and founded the Moreira Salles Institute, which is now home to one of the most comprehensive photographic exhibitions on the history of Rio de Janeiro. It is also the largest private photography collection in all of Brazil. The Institute regularly hosts a robust series of exciting events and exhibits of paintings and sculptures.

The Moreira Salles Institute is housed in the banker's former home, which was designed by the grand masters of Brazilian architecture, Architect Olavo Redig de Campos and Landscape Architect Burle Marx. The garden, with its masterfully deployed design features, deserves particular attention – do spend a little extra time here. Burle Marx plays with perspectives and refined materials in a most magnificent manner. A special gem and unique in its own way is Burle Marx' wall design featuring 4,016 blue and white tiles over a surface of 88 square meters. The motifs on this work of art are washerwomen and fish, and the tiles were manufactured in 1949 in the same factory that produced the fantastic panel by Candido Portinari in the Ministry for Education and Health.

In the pond, which reflects the tiles, carp and turtles swim, and water lilies and reeds thrive. The atmosphere here is dignified and romantic and often serves as the backdrop for receptions and exhibition openings.

Address Instituto Moreira Salles, Rua Marques de Sao Vicente 476, Gavea, Rio de Janeiro, RJ 22451-041, +55 (21) 3284 7400 www.ims.com.br/ims | **Getting there** Bus 170 to Rua Marq De Sao Vicente próximo ao 380 | **Hours** Tue–Sun 11am–8pm | **Tip** In the bookshop there are beautiful illustrated books on Brazilian photography and the architecture of the house.

76 __ The Museum of Astronomy
The Southern Cross

The Southern Cross is pretty much the only constellation in the southern sky that is also well known among inhabitants of the northern hemisphere as a symbol of the far-away, the fantastic, and the mysterious.

Originally built between 1913 and 1921 as the National Observatory, this site is now home to the Museum of Astronomy and Related Sciences (Museu de Astronomia e Ciencias Afins, or MAST), an institution that focuses on research into celestial bodies. The museum itself features an impressive exhibition on the history of astronomy, and the complex is one of the largest museums of its type in Latin America. The collection of astronomical instruments on view at MAST, some of which are from the National Observatory, includes historical timepieces that were used to determine the official time in Brasilia.

Three historical pavilions in the grounds of the museum contain gigantic telescopes from the early 19th century, which, at the time, were very much state-of-the-art in the field of stargazing.

Visitors also have the chance to use these high-tech devices to look at the Southern Cross in the "Stargazing Program." It starts with a museum employee giving a short introduction to the constellations of the southern hemisphere. Then, after nightfall the dome of the pavilion opens, and on clear days the night sky sparkles in all its glory. Participants can experience and easily identify the constellations they've just learned about with the help of one of the telescopes. The diameter of the lens, the light-gathering medium, is an important factor in what one can actually see. The larger the lens – and there are lenses with diameters of between 21 and 46 centimeters here – the more light it gathers and concentrates. In this way, weak stars, nebulae, and star clusters can be made out, that otherwise remain hidden to the naked eye. Fantastic!

Address Museu de Astronomia e Ciências Afins (MAST), Rua General Bruce 586, São Cristóvão, Rio de Janeiro, RJ 20921-030, +55 (21) 35145229, www.mast.br, atendimento@mast.br | **Getting there** Metro to São Cristóvão, then walk through the Quinta da Boa Vista Imperial Park (about 30 minutes) | **Hours** Tue–Fri 9am–5pm, Sat, Sun, & holidays 2–6pm, "Programa de Observação do Céu" (Stargazing Program) Wed & Sat after nightfall, 5:30–9pm on clear day, tours in English by reservation at atendimento@mast.br | **Tip** In the garden you will find a scaled model of the solar system, which makes for an interesting walk.

77__The Music Bookshop

Where bottles flew to bossa nova

The drinking and music-making went on into the early hours of the morning when a new music style was created here in the narrow streets of Copacabana. But this genesis hardly interested the neighbors – on the contrary, they were completely exasperated and resorted to throwing bottles at the noisy night owls. Since then, the corner bar in Copacabana has been called *Beco das Garrafas*, or the Bottle Lane. At the beginning of the bossa nova boom in the early 1960s, the great musicians such as João Gilberto and Tom Jobim played in three small bars: Little Club, Bacarat, and Bottles Bar.

As bossa nova later made its way around the world, musicians started performing on larger stages, and the small music bars ultimately degenerated into porn clubs, which were also known as "blow rooms" due to the particular service available to sex tourists. After elaborate restoration work, a commemorative plaque now adorns the street with the inscription, *Beco das Garrafas*. Bottle's Bar has live music on weekends again. The interior is identical to the way it was back in the early days, although the music is no longer the same.

But if you really want to immerse yourself in the world of bossa nova, you will find a real treasure trove in the biggest music bookshop in Brazil, with 2,500 books, from musicians' biographies and music history to song books. The CD collection comprises 4,000 disks with works of MPB (Música Popular Brasileira) as well as cinema soundtracks. A vinyl collection with rarities also invites experts to have a good rummage. Alongside guitars and drums – all of the very best quality for the professional musician – there are also loads of odds and ends, including mouse pads, T-shirts, and pens with bossa nova emblems. The exhibition about the genesis of the record "Canção do Amor Demais" by Vinícius de Moraes and Tom Jobim tells of the birth of bossa nova.

Address Bossa Nova e Companhia, Rua Duvivier 37, Copacabana, Rio de Janeiro, RJ 22020-020, +55 (21) 2295-8096, www.bossanovaecompanhia.com.br, contato@bossanovaecia.com.br | **Getting there** Metro to Cardeal Arcoverde | **Hours** Mon–Fri 9am–7pm, Sat 9am–5pm | **Tip** You can find sensational cakes at Biscuit Doces e Salgados (Rua Carvalho de Mendonça 35, Copacabana, Rio de Janeiro, RJ 22020-050).

78 — The Music School in Urca
Orchestra rehearsal is on Saturdays

It starts to get a little noisy on the university campus in the sedate neighborhood of Urca from 11:30am on Saturday mornings, when students, along with older musicians, meet with guitars, cellos, and flutes in the enchanting garden, gathering together in small groups before beginning to rehearse. They only receive the notes for the orchestra rehearsal that morning – a challenge for many, especially those who are new to the music.

These are students of the Escola Portátil de Música, which has existed in this form since 2000 and was set up by great Brazilian musicians in order to teach the original Brazilian *choro*. This music style goes back to the 1870s in Rio de Janeiro, as a fusion of popular European music such as polka and the waltz with the music of African slaves. It is practically considered the first uniquely Brazilian music style, a precursor, so to speak, of samba and bossa nova. The most famous representative is the composer Heitor Villa-Lobos, for whom *choro* is the essence and the soul of Brazilian music. *Choro* experienced renewed interest at the start of this century. The film *Brasileirinho* by Mika Kaurismäki, which was premiered in Berlin in 2005, made the music style famous around the world.

To this day, *choro* serves as an inspiration to singers of MPB (Popular Brasilian Music). Almost every great Brazilian musician went through the school of *choro*. After its beginnings with 50 pupils, the institute now already has over 1,000 students and almost 30 teachers. The *Bandão*, as the open air orchestra rehearsal on Saturdays at the foot of the Urca hill is called, is free, and everyone is welcome. When the conductor takes up the baton at around noon, it takes a while until everyone has settled down and found their places. But then you will feel *choro* "right down into your pores and your soul" – many loyal listeners know the feeling well.

Address Bandão da Escola Portátil de Música, Avenida Pasteur 436, Urca, Rio de Janeiro, RJ 22290-240, +55 (21) 2242-3597, www.escolaportatil.com.br, cross over the courtyard | **Getting there** Metro to Botafogo, then bus 513, for example, to Avenida Pasteur próximo ao 458 | **Hours** Sat 12.30–1.30pm, but you are welcome to arrive earlier and can listen to the students practicing | **Tip** The Museu de Ciências da Terra, Earth Sciences Museum, is housed in a majestic building very close by (Av. Pasteur 404, 2º Andar, Urca, Rio de Janeiro, RJ 22290-255).

79__Musicians' Corner

Homesick for Portugal!

During the week, only a few tables are occupied in the Cantinho das Concertinas, or Musicians Corner, as laborers from the area eat lunch here beside the CADEG market hall. But come Saturday, the atmosphere is festive, everything is decorated with Portuguese and Brazilian flags, instruments wait on a stage, and often all the tables are filled by 11am.

There are *bacalhau,* or codfish, balls; baked codfish with potatoes, garlic, and black olives; or sardines with boiled potatoes – all national dishes of Portugal – and, of course, beer. Dessert is Portuguese sweets, all delicious.

The guests are mostly Portuguese originally. Most of them came to Brazil in the 1960s during the dictatorship of António Salazar, which came to an end with the rebellion of large parts of the army in the Carnation Revolution of 1974.

This was also the reason that owner Carlos Cadavez left his home in northern Portugal at the age of just 14 years. In the beginning, he only cooked for close friends at the CADEG market. Traditionally, food, drinks, and flowers are sold here – all at cheap market prices. But the Portuguese specialties on offer at lunchtime have been just as famous since the 1970s. Carlos Cadavez's stall soon became popular amongst the Portuguese, and lunchtime eventually became nothing less than a party. For 15 years, the compatriots' get-together has taken place under the unofficial name of *Festa Portuguesa.*

It takes a while for the musicians to stir themselves, but then the accordion strikes up, and the band plays the first folk song from their homeland. And then it isn't long before the guests just can't bear to sit in their chairs any longer. Everyone dances with great passion: retired couples, young people, children with their grannies. The nostalgic party rolls on into the evening. Here, those who were once the occupiers of Brazil are now the immigrants.

Address O Cantinho das Concertinas, CADEG, Rua Capitão Félix 110, Rua 16, Benfica, Rio de Janeiro, RJ 20920-900 | **Getting there** Metro to São Cristóvão, then bus 665 to Rua Prefeito Olimpio De Melo próximo ao 1531, taxi, or around 15-minutes' walk | **Hours** Sat from noon | **Tip** If you decide to go by foot, marvel at the downright pompous military hospital (Rua Francisco Manoel 126, Benfica, Rio de Janeiro, RJ 20911-270) on the way there, and on the way back enjoy one of the best *chope* (draft beer) in the city at Bar Adonis (Rua São Luiz Gonzaga 2156A, Benfica, Rio de Janeiro, RJ 20910-062).

80 The Pasmado Vantage Point

Over the tunnel

Pasmado is one of 1,000 hills in the city, and one from which the view of Guanabara Bay is unparalleled. The *mirante*, or view, is particularly unique for several reasons. It is located in Parque Yitzhak Rabin, which is never very crowded. To the contrary, in fact, this is one of the most peaceful and idyllic places you will find between the lively streets of Copacabana and busy neighborhood of Botafogo.

The park is actually on the peak of the hill right in between the two neighborhoods. A 220-meter-long tunnel was drilled through the hill in the 1950s to connect these two areas, a complex project that took five years to complete. Up until the 1960s, the hill was home to a *favela*, but the police drove out the residents during the military dictatorship. The municipal authorities at the time promised that the residents would be assigned new accomodations, but critics are very doubtful these people ever received new homes.

Starting in 1965, a reforestation project began on the hill, and the park was revitalized with beautiful new plantings. The flame trees with their red springtime blossom are particularly striking. The view offers all of the Guanabara Bay classics: Corcovado, Morro da Urca, and Sugarloaf Mountain, as well as the tallest skyscraper in Rio de Janeiro, the Rio Sul Center, also known as *Torre Rio Sul*, which towers at 164 meters and 58 stories high as you look to the right.

The park is named after the Israeli prime minister and Nobel Peace Prize winner Yitzhak Rabin, and it is indeed a peaceful place. A small kiosk serves drinks and biscuits, and park benches invite you to sit and enjoy the tranquility and the remarkable details of the panoramic views, while life pulses in the metropolis below you. The peace and relative privacy also attracts many couples in the evening hours, who come up here to enjoy the romantic atmosphere.

Address Mirante do Pasmado, Parque Yitzhak Rabin, Botafogo, Rio de Janeiro, RJ 22290-240 | **Getting there** Any bus to Shopping Rio Sul, then taxi | **Hours** Unrestricted | **Tip** Fogo de Chão serves a fantastic *churrasco a rodizio*, with practically every kind of meat, an all-you-can-eat menu, and a salad buffet (Avenida Réporter Nestor Moreira, Botafogo, RJ 22290-210, www.fogodechao.com.br).

81___Paulo Dallier's Atelier
The van Gogh of Morro da Conceição

"I thought I was a Laurence Olivier or an Orson Welles, but in the end I followed Vincent van Gogh. I wrote photo-novelas and plays, and only started to paint at 39." At first, Paulo Dallier sold his naïve-style paintings in the hippie market in Ipanema. After six years, he found his own style: expressionist, sometimes abstract, and occasionally reminiscent of French Fauvism. His paintings cast a spell, with their powerful brushstrokes and their explosive colors.

The house of the now 86-year-old artist also serves as a gallery: pictures of *sambistas* (samba musicians and dancers) of São Jorge, the unofficial patron saint of the city (see ch. 45), circus scenes, and self-portraits hang on the walls.

His paintings have also been exhibited in the Centro Cultural Banco do Brasil as well as in Europe, while a film about his life was shown as part of the urban development project Porto Maravilha in 2016.

Dallier is deeply rooted in the district of Morro da Conceição, right next to the redesigned harbor, having grown up here. The streetscape has been influenced by the Portuguese since the 16th century – an oasis of peace in the hectic city center, hiding away the architectural treasures of "Old Rio," such as the Fortress of Conceição, the episcopal palace, and the hanging gardens of Valongo (see ch. 104).

Nowadays, Dallier is the unofficial mayor of the neighborhood. The windows of his little house remain open, while the artist receives visitors warmly – often in a T-shirt covered in splashes of paint – and shows them around his atelier, with magnificent views of the harbor from the kitchen. If you like, he will even take you on a walking tour. Twenty artists have settled here, joining together under the banner of the Project Mauá initiative, and once a year they all open their gates. Dallier's door, on the other hand, is always open.

Address Ladeira João Homem 52, Saúde, Rio de Janeiro, RJ 20081-130 52 | **Getting there** Metro to Uruguaiana, then walk along Avenida Rio Branco towards the harbor, left onto Rua Acre, the first right onto Travessa do Liceu, and then up the stairs on the right into Ladeira João Homem | **Hours** Variable | **Tip** In Imaculada Bar & Galeria, at number 7 on the same street, you'll find good food served in a pleasant atmosphere, and often an art exhibition to boot (www.barimaculada.com.br).

82 __ The Pavilion in Sepetiba

Promises from politicians

Mayor Odorico Paraguaçu has big plans: the opening of the cemetery should give his political career a real boost. But it's taking time – no one in the village thinks about dying. Under pressure from the opposition, the mayor makes plans to defeat them and commissions a killer, but he botches his mission. And then there's Doroteia, Dulcineia, and Judiceia, his three secretaries and lovers, in short: Sodom and Gomorrah in Sucupira, the fictitious city in the State of Bahia.

This was the premise of the first full-color telenovela, *O Bem-Amado*, which premiered in 1973, based on the novel by Dias Gomes. During the filming, the mayor delivered his speeches from a pavilion on the square in Sepetiba, a fishing and swimming resort around 70 kilometers/44 miles west of Rio's city center.

Originally, Rio's first pavilion stood on the Praça XV in the city center, erected in 1903 in the course of the urban reforms of Mayor Pereira Passos. It could hold up to 80 musicians, and the marine orchestra played at its inauguration. Later, this splendid specimen was brought to Sepetiba. There are a total of 21 such pavilions in Rio.

As much as the rural atmosphere back then corresponded to life in Bahia, this spot now seems like a relic from the past. Gallant egrets walk along the shore, and if the bay were only not so polluted – the ThyssenKrupp Steelworks near the deep-water harbor was in the headlines for years, and the smell on the beach is still noticeable – it would be a magical bathing resort. The bay once competed with the Copacabana as the "Princess in the Southwest." The view is still idyllic, but the rest is unfortunately an environmental disaster.

This pavilion was inaugurated in 1949. Here too a politician made a speech and promised the citizens a fantastic future. Everyone has long since forgotten. The cemetery in the telenovela was never built after all.

Address Praça Washington Luís, Sepetiba, Rio de Janeiro, RJ 23545-046 | **Getting there** Train from Central to Santa Cruz, then bus 2304 (a total of around 2 hours) to Sepetiba | **Tip** There is a large statue of the sea goddess Iemanjá in the bay. February 2 is her feast day, which the community celebrates with a rousing celebration.

83 Penha Basilica
On the observation post

The two towers of the Nossa Senhora da Penha Basilica are widely visible from all around. The church was built high up on the rocks by a Portuguese sailor in the 17th century. A total of 382 stairs lead up to it, and legend has it that it was hewn straight out of the rocks at the behest of a faithful woman named Maria Barbosa, in thanks for heeding her prayers. In 1819 she gave birth to a healthy son after years of childlessness.

The church continues to be a place of pilgrimage to this day. Many signs of thanks in the *sala dos milagres*, or hall of miracles, bear witness the many ways "Our Lady of Penha" has come to the aid of believers: school reports, wheelchairs, marriage certificates, wax arms and legs, birth certificates, locks of hair to fulfill a wish.

The plain beauty of the church itself is impressive. If you look down into the valley you can see one *favela* merging into another, and on the horizon you should be able to make out Sugarloaf Mountain. In the past, the feared Comando Vermelho, Rio's biggest criminal organization, literally called the shots here. A few years ago things came to a head with a spectacular occupation of the Complexo do Alemão, one of the city's largest *favela* complexes, by the military police. The shooting went on for days. On the news, viewers could watch live footage taken from helicopters as the drug bosses fled the city. Today, the gang's presence can no longer be felt, although the violence returned conspicuously after the 2016 Olympic Games. However, the reputation of the military police is also not spotless, and some residents think they are worse than the gangsters.

Even though shootings are reported time and again, this trip, especially on a Sunday when many people come to the church, is quite safe. The transport connections are good, and the opportunity to take a closer look at another aspect of Rio is unique.

Address Nossa Senhora da Penha, Largo da Penha 19, Penha, Rio de Janeiro, RJ 21070-560, +1 (55) 21 3219-6262, www.santuariopenhario.org.br | **Getting there** Train from Central (platform 12) to Penha, Mon–Sat about every five minutes, less frequent on the weekend (www.supervia.com.br/servicos-supervia) take the right exit to Rua José Mauricio, through the pedestrian zone, left at the end and then follow the signs to Santuário da Penha. *Carioca* Ivo Korytowski offers guided tours in the area (ivokory@gmail.com) | **Hours** Basilica Sun & Sat 7am–6pm, Hall of Miracles Sun 7am–noon, see website for mass schedule | **Tip** On the first Saturday in October there is an impressive event with a procession on the Feast of Nossa Senhora da Penha.

84 The Península Residential Area

Like living in Miami

The remote neighborhood of Barra da Tijuca became popular because there is a beautiful beach here, the longest one in Rio in fact, and rent for apartments and houses was initially reasonable in comparison with Copacabana. The production company for the TV station Rede Globo is not too far away in Jacarepaguá, film stars followed suit, and soon life in the skyscraper development in Barra became cool.

The Península Complex on the edge of Lagoa da Tijuca, or Tijuca Lake – all built sustainably according to the plans of Mário Moscatelli, a biology professor at Santa Úrsula University – perfectly serves the Brazilian need for security. Here people live in *condominios*, closed-off apartment blocks, with a concierge! Anyone who cannot provide ID is not allowed to enter the building. A very comforting feeling.

Península has cultivated this lifestyle: around 15,000 people live in the 55 skyscrapers built to date on an area of around 780,000 square meters, with supermarkets, restaurants, and shopping malls. Only eight percent of the ground area is built on! The ambience conveys luxury, and the Venetian lions at the entrance send a clear signal: those who live here are in a class of their own. The sale price of around €3,000 per square meter of living area can certainly compete with the major cities of Europe.

Although security guards control access to the complex with a barrier, anyone can enter, as the streets are public space. So you're completely entitled to take a walk through this world of its own as a humble visitor. It has its own bus, and cats roam through the lawns. There are five themed gardens to choose from – the sculpture park perhaps? Life here almost appears unreal in its loftiness. There are even young people who grow up here in Barra and only see the center of Rio for the first time when they start working.

Address Condominio Península, Rua Bauhíneas da Península 150, Barra da Tijuca, Rio de Janeiro, RJ 22776-090 | **Getting there** Bus to Barra Shopping, for example 361 from Carioca or 614 from Del Castilho or 315 from Central, then taxi (or, when it's finished, metro to Jardim) | **Tip** The *batidas* in Bar do Oswaldo in the Barrinha neighborhood, at the beginning of the original Barra, are legendary, with *caffè crema*, coconut, and *açaí* among others (Estrada do Joá 3896, Joá, Rio de Janeiro, RJ 22611-022, www.bardooswaldo.com.br, weekdays noon–1am, weekend noon–3am).

85 — The Police Palace

Former torture chamber

The Palácio da Polícia, or Police Palace, is certainly awe-inspiring! 6,000 square meters/65,000 square feet in size, it was built in 1910 as the central headquarters for the Police Department when Rio de Janeiro was the capital of Brazil. The award-winning architect Heitor de Mello (1875–1920) designed the monumental building, which now belongs to the cultural heritage of the city, in an eclectic style.

Through two dictatorships, and during Getúlio Vargas' regime, which was, in truth, an autocracy, the Palácio was the place from which the state exercised control. This building was where political opponents were detained, interrogated, and systematically tortured.

The citizens of Rio also called it *Prédio do Dops*, the building of the "Department for Political and Social Order" (Departamento de Ordem Política e Social, DOPS), the notoriously repressive organ of the military dictatorship that operated here from 1924 to 1983.

As a result of the work carried out by the Truth Commission on the military dictatorship's human rights abuses, there have been efforts to create a political museum in the Police Palace. "We mustn't forget. This building is predestined to be a memorial against repression, the museum to become a cult for democracy," the concluding report says.

The commission was initiated through the efforts of former President Dilma Rousseff, who was, herself, tortured during the dictatorship as a fighter in the armed resistance against the military police in the neighborhood of Tijuca (see ch. 34).

After the end of the dictatorship in 1985, the civil police moved into the building. There is actually already a museum here that is currently being restored and is temporarily accommodated in an outbuilding. The exhibits include uniforms from the time when Rio de Janeiro was the capital, objects and utensils from police work, and manhunt records.

Address Palacio da Policia, Rua da Relação 40, Rio de Janeiro, RJ 20231-110 | **Getting there** Metro to Carioca | **Hours** Mon–Fri 11am–5.30pm | **Tip** Once a month, the Cordão da Bola Preta Samba School hold its Feijoada da Bola Preta, a raucus dinner and samba party, on Saturdays starting at noon. See website for dates and details (Rua da Relação 3, Lapa, Rio de Janeiro, RJ 2023 1110, www.cordaodabolapreta.com).

86 Prainha Park
A life in the treetops

Sloths spend almost their entire lives in trees. They have long, curved claws that grow up to 10 centimeters in length with which they hang from the branches – that is their standard position. And it's actually the position in which they do everything – sleep, eat, procreate, and give birth. They climb down only once every one to two weeks to heed nature's call. Their metabolism is so slow that this is completely sufficient. Why they have to get down from the trees for this of all things still puzzles researchers to this day.

You can therefore consider yourself quite lucky if you discover one moving through the treetops in slow motion or indeed climbing down to the ground while you're on a walk through the Parque Natural Municipal da Prainha, which grants this most primeval and simultaneously most peculiar mammal of the New World a special sanctuary. The nature park has existed on 147 hectares since 2001, and it is also home to wild cats and dogs, various monkey species, hummingbirds and parrots, and many indigenous snakes, as well as nocturnal animals.

The path to the viewing point Mirante do Caeté leads through the lush vegetation of the Atlantic Rainforest, with its unique fauna. Some of the species of trees are threatened with extinction, such as the *pau brasil* (Brazilwood). Orchids blossom in the trees; time and again you will see bright orange colored flowers gleaming among the leaves. Once you reach the highest point, you will be rewarded with a superb panoramic view of the seemingly endless sandy beaches of the Recreio dos Bandeirantes region, with some bizarre stone formations.

Just opposite the park is the wild Prainha Beach, famous among surfers for its fantastic waves. This place is pretty busy on the weekends, and surf competitions regularly take place, but on a weekday you can generally savor the exquisite bay between the rocks in absolute peace.

Address Parque Natural Municipal da Prainha, Avenida Estado da Guanabara 58, Recreio dos Bandeirantes, Rio de Janeiro, RJ 22790-852 | **Getting there** Bus 2334 or 2335 to Recreio dos Bandeirantes, then by taxi; there is no public transport to this beach, but there's a surfer bus in the summertime | **Hours** Tue–Sun 8am–5pm | **Tip** Only a few kilometers further on you can enjoy excellent fish for lunch right by the sea at Mirante da Prainha (Av. Estado da Guanabara 689, Recreio dos Bandeirantes, Rio de Janeiro, RJ 22790-852).

87__The Rubem Braga Complex

Like a bridge between rich and poor

Right next to the General Osório metro station, just a short distance from the beach at Ipanema, panorama elevators in the Rubem Braga building complex lead to Mirante da Paz, or Viewing Point of Peace. The view of Ipanema and Leblon Beaches, Morro Dois Irmãos, the lagoon, Corcovado, and the Cagarras Islands is stunning!

But many who use the elevator are less interested in the panoramic views than they are in simply getting to the top, where a bridge-like passage leads to the complex's second tower. They proceed to the facing hill, to their homes in the *favelas* of Cantagalo and Pavão / Pavãozinho (see ch. 43). There are few places in the city where one can experience so directly the proximity, and at the same time the gulf, between a *comunidade*, or a community, as the residents of the *favelas* up on the hill call themselves, and *asfalto* (asphalt), as they call the tawny residential and beach areas of the rich and beautiful people down below. The city built a literal and metaphorical bridge between the two and now, visitors and residents of Ipanema get to enjoy the view that was previously reserved for the *favela* residents up in the hills. In return, the residents of Cantagalo can now reach the metro station within minutes.

The complex, named after the journalist Rubem Braga, was inaugurated in 2010. For its construction, a tunnel 260 meters or 285 yards long was excavated out of the rock, connecting the taller of the two towers (64 meters/210 feet and 31 meters/102 feet, respectively) with the General Osório metro station. Thousands of people benefit daily from this "means of transport." Previously, they had to descend and ascend over 400 stairs in order to get to work and home again. At the inauguration, the mayor of Rio called the project a contribution to social integration.

Address Rua Barão da Torre 66, Rio de Janeiro, RJ 22411-003 | **Getting there** Metro to General Osório | **Hours** Daily 5am–11pm | **Tip** The legendary Feira Hippie, or Hippie Fair market takes place every Sunday on the square in front of the metro station (Praça General Osório, Ipanema, Rio de Janeiro, RJ 20410-020, www.feirahippieipanema.com).

88 __ Runway 02
Landing on a very short runway

The approach from São Paulo to runway 02 of the Santos Dumont airport is spectacular – like a free sightseeing tour of Rio as a welcoming gift. First the mountains, then the bay, the sea, and the Sugarloaf – a beautiful dream!

But if you look at the runway during approach, it will make you catch your breath – it looks as if the airplane were landing right in the sea. You can experience the challenging landing from the cockpit on video – search for "Santos Dumont Pista O2" on Youtube if you dare.

Runway 02 is only 1,323 meters (1,447 yards) long and touches the Guanabara Bay at both ends. Landing on a glide path, as is otherwise customary, is impossible here, as Sugarloaf Mountain is only four kilometers away from the runway. Instead, pilots have to fly in towards the chain of cliffs, taking a tight turn to the left before landing. The smallest mistake by the pilot, and a water landing is unavoidable! Sometimes this actually happens, for example in 2010, when a taxi plane landed in the Atlantic. On the other hand, taxis that bring military personnel to the base right next to the runway have to make leeway for runway 02. The road goes right past the end of the runway – if drivers gets the timing wrong, they could be whirled through the air by the power of the turbines. Although warning signs identify the area as a security zone long before the runway, curious people line up time and again nearby to watch the landing maneuvers up close. But you should definitely stay away from the runway itself.

The airport is a real viewing platform, on one side the Sugarloaf, *Christ the Redeemer*, and the Glória Marina, on the other the Rio–Niterói Bridge. Some visitors walk around here as if on a Sunday stroll, but the deafening sound of the turbines doesn't allow for contemplative activities. Watching aircraft here is an impressive spectacle and something of an adventure.

Address Praça Vereador Miguel Angelo, Centro, Rio de Janeiro, RJ 20021-340, exit Avenida Almirante Silvio de Noronha at the airport, +55 (21) 3814-7070, www.aeroportosantosdumont.net/en | **Getting there** Metro to Cinelândia, then with the new tram (VLT) to the end stop Santos Dumont; by car: exit Avenida Almirante Silvio de Noronha at the airport | **Tip** The two giant paintings (15 by 4 meters) by Cadmo Fausto in the airport lobby, with themes of human flight from Icarus to modern aircraft, are worth a look.

89 __ Saint Anastasia

The slave girl with the iron mask

She was proud and lovely; they say she inherited her unusual, radiant blue eyes from her mother, a beautiful Bantu princess. But in 1740, as a young girl, she was condemned to hide her beauty behind an iron mask. The slave girl Anastasia had become the object of her master's desire, but she refused to succumb to him. He raped her and had her fitted with an iron mask as punishment for her stubbornness and resistance.

To this day, Anastasia is a heroine in the resistance against slave owners and one of the most important female figures in Afro-Brazilian history. For her thousands of devotees, she is a saint, whose intercession they are counting on, even though the Catholic Church has never acknowledged Anastasia's ordeal.

For the devout who regularly ask Anastasia for assistance in the chapel to the right of the Igreja de Nossa Senhora do Rosário e São Benedito, or Church of Our Lady of the Rosary and Saint Benedict, the lack of official recognition seems to make no difference in their faith.

In 1968, in a church founded by a brotherhood of black Brazilians, an exhibition on the 80th anniversary of the abolition of slavery in Brazil launched Anastasia as a popular and powerful spiritual figure. Diverse representatives of Afro-Brazilian religions have repeatedly turned to the Pope, requesting that Anastasia be canonized. In 1984 there was even an official petition to the Vatican, which the Pope countered with a ban on Anastasia effigies, especially in the large Brazilian churches. A commission summoned by the Vatican determined that there was no empirical evidence for the existence of the slave girl Anastasia – the whole story was, apparently, just a myth.

Neverthless, the effigy of the martyr experienced a revival after a short time, and around 28 million devotees in the country still come to the slave girl in the iron mask with their wishes and prayers.

Address Nossa Senhora do Rosário e São Benedito, Rua Uruguaiana 77, Rio de Janeiro, RJ 20050-094, +55 (21) 3176-3808, www.facebook.com/insrsbhp | **Getting there** Metro to Uruguaiana | **Tip** Above the church is the Museu do Negro with exhibits on slavery, emancipation, and black identity in Brazil (R. Uruguaiana, 77, Centro, Rio de Janeiro, RJ 20050-094, www.facebook.com/museudonegro.rio).

90 Santa Cruz da Barra Fortress

The Alcatraz of the tropics

Ferocious waves and breakers wash around the six-meter-thick walls, completely cut-off from land – for centuries rebels were imprisoned here, and escape was almost impossible. For the United States, it was Alcatraz in the San Francisco Bay; for Brazil, it was Santa Cruz da Barra in Rio's Guanabara Bay.

The French laid the foundations of this mighty fortress in 1555, with the intention of protecting the entry to the Guanabara Bay from enemies. Together with São João Fortress on the other side of the bay in the neighborhood of Urca, and the da Laje Fortress, the Santa Cruz Fortress created an impenetrable line of defense against invaders.

Nonetheless, the French buccaneer Jean-François Duclerc and his men attacked Rio de Janeiro in 1710. However, the attempt to march into the city on foot failed. Duclerc and his men were imprisoned – he perished under circumstances that have remained unknown.

Among his men was Gaston Raymond de la Salle, the only one who managed to escape – in an act fit for the movies. The jail cells were below sea-level and damp. More rats lived here than prisoners, many of whom died of pneumonia and cholera. Raymond – weakened by months in the dark cell – jumped into the sea from the walls of the prison. The risk of hitting the rocks and being swallowed up by the foaming waves was great, but he managed to swim to a boat that took him across to land on the other side of the bay. Nothing is known of how he managed to leave his cell and get over the wall. What we do know for certain is that he later showed up again in France.

Today, the prison, in which common criminals as well as rebels, and later political prisoners, served their sentences, is a museum. Because of its breathtaking location, the view across the bay is enthralling, with all the beauties of Rio de Janeiro's coastline in full view.

Address Fortaleza de Santa Cruz da Barra, Estrada General Eurico Gaspar Dutra, Jurujuba, Niterói, Rio de Janeiro, RJ 2710-2354 | **Getting there** Ferry from Praça XV to Niterói, then taxi to the fort or bus 33 from the bus terminal to the last stop. The route to the fort leads past small, enchanting fishing bays that are simply begging to be swam in. | **Hours** Tue–Sun 10am–5pm, only on guided tours in groups | **Tip** At the Parque da Cidade you will find a 300-meter-high paragliding ramp. The view of the bay from the top is breathtaking (Estrada da Viração, s/n, São Francisco, Niterói, RJ 26177-600).

91 Santa Marta Favela
Community, caipirinha, and Cristo

Thiago Firmino always waits inside Select, the bar in the gas station opposite the entrance to the Santa Marta Favela. He was born in Santa Marta and organizes tours through his neighborhood. "In the past," he explains, "we waited here until dawn. Walking up by foot at night was much too dangerous." The *favela* was the first to be pacified in 2008, and the cable car ride up to the top now saves you from walking the 788 stairs up or down.

On the platform of the last of five stops, the view stretches from Botafogo to Guanabara Bay, Sugarloaf, and the Corcovado with *Christ the Redeemer*, arms open wide. From no other viewing point in the city will you get so close to this iconic symbol of Rio at the same height.

Thiago says that not all of the houses in Santa Marta have been legalized – there are no documents for those in the upper section. "Area of risk" is the official term, and speculation is already in full swing. Some 1,700 families live here in 650 houses, through narrow alleyways past open windows, down to the place where Michael Jackson shot the video for "They Don't Care About Us" in 1996. On Saturdays a *feijoada* with samba music takes place here at sunset. Thiago himself lives a bit further down. At his place, it's time for *caipirinhas* and stories about the *comunidade*, the "community," as the inhabitants call their *favela*. In recent years there has been something of an economic boom: there is now a beauty salon, a football pitch, and some of the restaurants, such as Pizza do Luiz, have even made it into the foodie columns of the dailies.

The brightly colored Praça Cantão back down at the bottom is a pleasant surprise – the Dutch art duo Haas & Hahn have covered 7,000 square meters of the façades of 34 houses in rainbow colors and geometric shapes as part of the art project, "Favela Painting." The everyday life of the community plays out in front of this backdrop.

Address Rua São Clemente, near Praça Curumbá, Rio de Janeiro, RJ 22260-130, the bar in the gas station, Select, is the meeting point, info and tours at favelasantamartatour.blogspot.com, also in English | **Getting there** Metro to Botafogo | **Tip** Thiago Firmino also organizes nighttime tours with a *churrasco*, or a Brazilian barbecue, and a climb to a fantastic viewing point over the bay (www.favelasantamartatour.blogspot.com). The sunset is stunning from here. Enquire for details at favelasantamartatour@yahoo.com.br.

92 Santana Plaza

Wondrous park

The English-style park Campo de Santana, or Santana Plaza, is located in the middle of the city center, bordering the busy Saara business district (see ch. 17) but everyone seems to pass by it in a rush. The artfully forged gate is a promise of an enchanting alternative.

Inside the park, there are five specimens of the baobab tree, which grow towards the heavens, it would seem, in bizarre shapes. The park also contains the tallest baobab tree in all of Brazil, at 25 meters. The trees look mysterious and may remind you of the story *The Little Prince* by Antoine de Saint-Exupéry, in which baobab trees threaten recklessly to overgrow their small planet.

There are only a few baobabs, which originally come from Madagascar, in the whole of Brazil. When they were planted here in the mid-18th century, this was the border between the city of Rio de Janeiro and the surrounding countryside.

The park got its name from a nearby church, which was forced to make way for the first railway station in 1854. Today, the Estação Central do Brasil (Brazil's Central Station) is on the other side of the square.

The most important event on the Campo de Santana was the proclamation of the Brazilian Republic in 1889. A memorial in the middle of the park reminds us of the big day. A walk through the park will take you along atmospheric paths, around little lakes, and over bridges to man-made caves and an art garden. The landscape architect was Auguste Glaziou, who designed several gardens in Rio including the famous Passeio Público.

The park is well known among Cariocas because of its horde of cheeky residents, the *cutias*, a South American species of rodent that looks like a squirrel without the bushy tail. They stride, trot, gallop, and even jump high in the air, living in peaceful coexistence with the cats and pigeons in the park – they are strict vegetarians.

Address Praça da República, Centro, Rio de Janeiro, RJ 20211-351 | **Getting there** Metro to Uruguaiana or Carioca, it is not advisable to use the entrance / exit on the side of the Central station, as this isn't a particularly peaceful area, even during the day | **Hours** Daily 9am–5pm | **Tip** There are traditional partner dances at Gafieira Elite dance hall on the weekends (Rua Frei Caneca 4, Centro, Rio de Janeiro, RJ 20211-030).

93__São Cristóvão Football Club

Where Ronaldo kicked out at age 15

You can read "Aqui nasceu o Fenômeno" ("This is where Fenômeno was born"), written on the wall of the metro station, as the train heads out from the city center to Maracanã. The big letters are written on the outside of the stadium of the small soccer club, São Cristóvão. "Fenômeno" is Ronaldo Luís Nazário de Lima, known as Ronaldo, and this is where he first kicked a leather ball on a big pitch. As one of the greatest midfielders in the history of world soccer, he later sprinted and dribbled past the opposition, leaving some of the best in his wake.

Because the club's fame is limited – it currently plays in the Série B 1 – Cariocas only know of it because of Ronaldo. He came from a simple family in the outskirts. Even as a boy, he was more likely to be seen kicking a ball in the street than at his school desk. One day, he was invited to visit the soccer club, Valqueire Tênis Clube. There was no position available for him in the outfield, so Ronaldo had to play in goal. On his first game in the outfield, he scored four of the five goals, and soon after he began playing for a club in the Carioca League.

But his heart beat for Flamengo. He applied along with 400 other boys and was taken on. But he couldn't afford the ticket from the outskirts to Flamengo and had to drop out of the club. So Ronaldo ended up at São Cristóvão, who were willing to pay his travel costs. São Cristóvão sold him after two years, at the age of 15, for only US$7,500 in 1992, but the club of his youth went on to receive millions from later transfer fees from Real Madrid and Inter Milan in accordance with FIFA statues. During the 2014 World Cup, fans from Argentina, Spain, Columbia, and Japan came to take a look at the club, and Youth Coach Renato Campos, was happy to show them around. Now the motto here is "Fenômeno na bola, 10 na escola!" ("Phenomenal on the ball, top at school!").

Address São Cristóvão de Futebol e Regatas, Rua Figueira de Melo 200, Rio de Janeiro, RJ 20941-000 | **Getting there** Metro to São Cristóvão, then bus, for example 371 to Avenida Pedro II próximo ao 170-194 | **Hours** Mon–Fri 9am–5pm | **Tip** The National Museum of Brazil, the largest natural science and ethnological museum in Latin America, and it is, is well worth a visit (Quinta da Boa Vista, São Cristóvão, Rio de Janeiro, RJ 20940-040, www.museunacional.ufrj.br).

94__São José Market
Iconic happy hour

The only person here today is João, selling fruit and vegetables. Every day, the 80-year-old comes to the market from outside the city, where his family has a small plot of farmland.

At the time of imperial Brazil, there was a grain store in the simple hall, which would be filled by the nearby farm. In 1942, President Getúlio Vargas decided to establish a market in this location in order to provide the people of Rio with affordable food during World War II.

The building was neglected from the 1960s on. Then, after a long legal dispute, from which the residents of the neighborhood emerged victorious, the hall was landmarked in 1994 and officially became Mercado São José das Artes, the São José Art Market.

Apart from João's vegetable stall, things in the hall only start to get going from 6pm, as people meet up over a *chope* (draft beer) after work. The hall has blossomed into a cultural and culinary meeting point. Brazilian and international specialties are available at 16 stalls, there is space for 600 people on the tightly arranged tables, and the atmosphere quickly heats up.

Illustrious guests such as Brazil's most influential composer Tom Jobim have had glowing things to say about the venue. "The market is one of the friendliest places in the city, the people, the art, the music, the atmosphere, it's all reminiscent of the Rio of the good old days," he said. The carnival group Imprensa Que Eu Gamo was founded here in 1995 by a group of journalists over beers after work.

On Saturdays, there is an arts and crafts market from 10am to 5pm; there's live music on the last Saturday of the month; and on other days, there are often events in one of the bars, such as Botero (stalls 11, 12, and 13). The *petiscos*, or little snacks, such as turkey sausage with mini-onions and crispy potatoes, or the freshly baked pastry pockets, taste particularly good with a beer.

Address Mercadinho São José, Rua das Laranjeiras 90, on the corner of Rua Gago Coutinho, Laranjeiras, Rio de Janeiro, RJ 23094-025 | **Getting there** Metro to Largo do Machado | **Hours** Mon–Sat from 6pm, Sun from 1pm | **Tip** Right next to the metro station, you will find what many people consider to be the best codfish balls (*bohlino de bacalhau*) in the city at Adega Portugalia (Largo do Machado 30, Catete, Rio de Janeiro, RJ 22221-020, www.adegaportugalia.com.br/menu).

95 __ The Saracusas Fountain

Turtles from the convent

General Osório Square, in the middle of the chic neighborhood of Ipanema, is famous for its hippie fair flea market on Saturdays. It is busy here, right in front of the metro station, any day of the week. So you have to head determinedly to the middle of the square in order to be able to appreciate the antique fountain in its artistic entirety.

The top of the fountain is decorated with a cross, which had stood in the antique Convento da Ajuda, the Convent of Our Lady of Help, right up until the beginning of the 20th century, exactly where the Cinelândia Plaza is today, in the center of the city. It was the very first convent in Rio de Janeiro, built in 1795. The fountain is the work of Mestre Valentim, who is considered the greatest Brazilian artist from the period around the end of the 18th and start of the 19th century.

The multitalented Valentim was a sculptor, architect, and landscape architect, and he designed city-planning interventions such as the famous city park Passeio Público, where you'll see a fountain in the shape of a crocodile. The fountain in the courtyard of the convent primarily served as a water supply. An obelisk sits on top of a circular marble slab, and the water sprayed out of the bronze turtles that lay at the feet of the obelisk. This is also where the fountain gets its name "Saracusas," which is Portuguese for "turtles."

When, in 1911, the city center was expanding, the fountain was dismantled and reassembled in Ipanema. The turtles have been stolen on several occasions, the bronze sold for good money on the black market. The fountain has seen better days, but it's still fascinating. In 2015, the Geração Vidigal Fashion School chose the fountain as the location for their fashion show during Fashion Rio, where Rio de Janeiro's big design brands, such as Lenny Niemeyer and Patricia Viera presented their newest collections.

Address Praça General Osório, Ipanema, Rio de Janeiro, RJ 22410-020 | **Getting there** Metro to General Osório | **Tip** Close by, Felice Caffé serves great ice cream and delicious sandwiches (Rua Gomes Carneiro 20, Ipanema, Rio de Janeiro, RJ 22071-110, www.felice.com.br).

96_ The Sardine Triangle
Maritime chicken in Bar Ocidental

Perhaps the name was the idea of a guest who drew cartoons for a daily paper. The sight of the breadcrumb-coated sardine fillets that flew past him on plates made him spontaneously think of chicken breasts. And thus the *frango marítimo* (maritime chicken) was born.

The proprietor Fernando, on the other hand, remembers how, in the 1970s, a guest in the best of spirits after several ice-cold *chopes* (draft beers) made the joke of sticking a chicken foot between two sardines. The name is true to culinary history in any case: the sardine used to be the fish that everyone could afford, just like poultry is usually the cheapest meat.

No matter where the name came from, the Portuguese brothers Eduardo and Fernando have been serving sardines in the tradition of their homeland, open as fillets and not fried as whole fish, for over 50 years.

Back then, when there were still factories nearby, workers would come over for an affordable midday snack. The brothers soon opened a second bar, and they called it O Rei dos Frangos Marítimos (The King of Maritime Chicken). Today, there are five locations on the street, three of which belong to the brothers. The fried sardine has enjoyed a successful career as a delicacy. "The breadcrumbs are coarser than normal. We won't reveal the seasoning mix. The quality of the frying oil is also decisive – but everything actually depends on the perfect temperature of the oil in the fryer," Fernando says of the secret to their success.

You can sit at the tables outside by the road. The crispy fried sardines have even given the roadway a new name: Beco das Sardinhas (Sardine Triangle). The informal atmosphere has remained, along with the plain interior design and the good mood. Some people just stand around drinking cold beer – until their appetite is eventually and inevitably whetted, and they inevitably order a portion of *frango marítimo*.

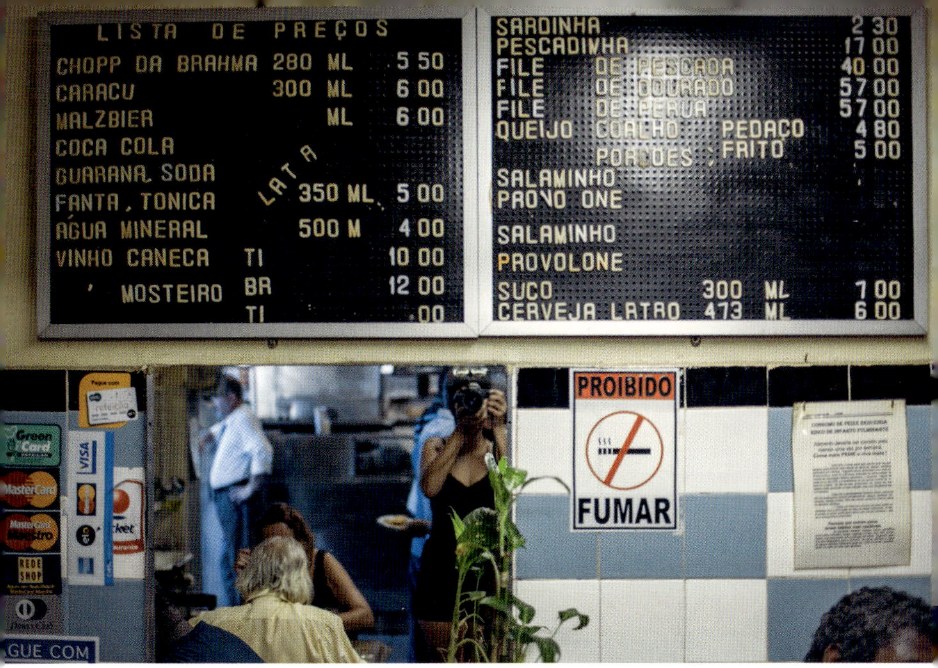
LISTA DE PREÇOS
CHOPP DA BRAHMA 280 ML 5 50
CARACU 300 ML 6 00
MALZBIER ML 6 00
COCA COLA
GUARANA. SODA
FANTA . TONICA
LATA
350 ML 5 00
ÁGUA MINERAL 500 M 4 00
VINHO CANECA TI 10 00
' MOSTEIRO BR 12 00
TI .00
SARDINHA 2 30
PESCADINHA 17 00
FILE DE PESCADA 40 00
FILE DE DOURADO 57 00
FILE DE PERUA 57 00
QUEIJO COALHO PEDAÇO 4 80
PORÇOES FRITO 5 00
SALAMINHO
PROVO ONE
SALAMINHO
PROVOLONE
SUCO 300 ML 7 00
CERVEJA LATAO 473 ML 6 00
PROIBIDO
FUMAR
GUE COM

Address Rua Miguel Couto 124, Loja C, between Rua Acre and Rua Visconde de Inhaúma, Rio de Janeiro, RJ 20070-030, +55 (21) 2253-4042, business.google.com/website/bar-ocidental | Getting there Metro to Uruguaiana | Hours Mon–Fri 8am–9pm, Sat 9am–4pm | Tip The bookstore Livraria da Travessa has a comprehensive range of titles, including many books about the City of Rio (Avenida Rio Branco 44, Centro, Rio de Janeiro, RJ 20090-002, www.travessa.com.br).

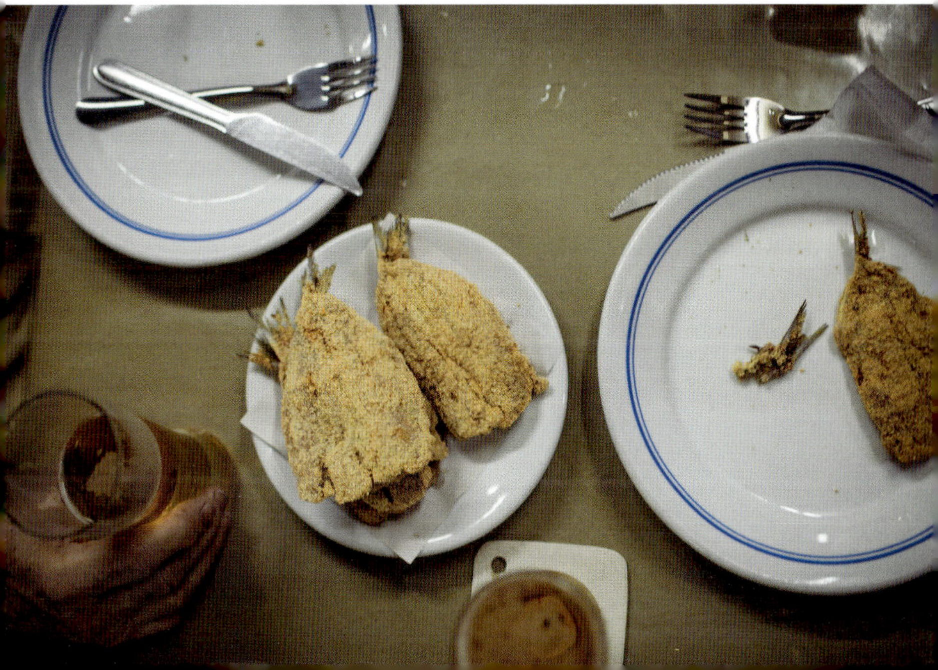

97 The Ship of Knowledge
Enterprise for digital citizens

Madureira is 30 kilometers outside of Rio de Janeiro, but due to the good train connection, it only takes 30 minutes to get there. The dressage tournaments in the 2016 Olympics also took place close by.

So much has changed. Until a few years ago, this area was the desolate outskirts of town, and there was very little for young people to do. Madureira Park, which hosts the biggest skateboard park in the city, as well as a sustainablility project with beautiful hanging gardens, now gives the area an ultra-modern image. In the middle of it all, as if it has just landed from outer space, is the Nave do conhecimento, or "Ship of Knowledge".

"From digital inclusion to social inclusion!" was former Mayor Eduardo Paes' motto for the "ship's" educational offerings. In total, there are six of these facilities in the outer regions of the city. The intention is to give citizens the opportunity to educate themselves digitally, develop creatively, and advance professionally. There are courses in computer graphics, video production, photography, and much more.

For those who can't handle a mouse, there's a workshop in digital literacy. The aim is to introduce people to the world of technology, but also to their rights as citizens. The Ship of Knowledge won the 2015 Architizer A+ international architecture award in New York. Designs from over 100 countries were submitted, and Architect Dietmar Stark's project for Rio came out on top in the audience vote, above Belgium and Italy, among others. "If the facilities fill citizens with enthusiasm, they will also be interested in the space, and once you step foot into the building, you will become interested in what is being offered," said Stark during the inauguration.

Two years after the opening of the "Ship," the city has recorded more than one million visitors, many of whom have now already completed courses.

Address Nave do Conhecimento, Parque de Madureira, at Rua Manuel Marquês, Madureira, Rio de Janeiro, RJ 20220-281, www.pracadoconhecimento.org.br | **Getting there** Train Supervia from Central to Madureira, check the schedule at: www.supervia.com.br | **Hours** Tue – Sat 9am – 9pm, Sun 9.30am – 4.30pm | **Tip** The hotdogs from Doggies just next door are delicious – you should definitely try the Classic.

98 The Soldiers' Memorial

Smoking snakes

South America is well known as a haven for Nazi supporters who fled Europe after WWII. The notorious Josef Mengele hid in Brazil until his death. Nonetheless, Brazil was the only South American country to fight against Hitler's regime.

"It's more likely for a snake to smoke a pipe, than for Brazil to take part in the war in Europe," had been the stance for a long time. After all, the president at the time, Getúlio Vargas, had looked up to Italy's fascist leader Mussolini as a role model when proclaiming the *Estado Novo*, the New State in Brazil, after the *coup d'etat* of 1937. But things turned out differently, and so the Brazilian soldiers who were deployed in World War II called themselves "smoking snakes," and even wore an emblem with a pipe-smoking snake. By 1941, Brazil had granted the US Navy the right to use its Atlantic harbors. The Germans triggered war with Brazil in 1942, when German U-boats sank Brazilian freight ships and more than 600 seamen lost their lives. On July 2, 1944, the first 5,000 soldiers of the Força Expedicionária Brasileira, the Brazilian Expeditionary Forces, set off towards Europe. In the end, 25,000 men were deployed on European soil. They fought, for example, at the "Gothic Line" in Serchio Valley near Lucca, with the goal of driving the Nazi troops out of Italy. Winter in the Apennines was a dramatic experience for the Brazilians.

Altogether, 467 soldiers lost their lives in Italy, and this 30-meter memorial was erected in their honor. The three soldiers on the memorial symbolize a marine, a foot soldier, and a pilot. The whole memorial covers over 6,850 square meters on Aterro do Flamengo, with a breathtaking view of Guanabara Bay.

The soldiers were first buried in Pistoia in Italy, then transferred to Brazil in 1960, and buried in a mausoleum. This, as well as a small museum with weapons and texts from World War II, is open to visitors.

Address Monumento Nacional dos Mortos da Segunda Guerra Mundial, Avenida Infante Dom Henrique 75, Aterro do Flamengo, Rio de Janeiro, RJ 20021-140 | **Getting there** Metro to Flamengo | **Hours** Unrestricted from the outside; museum Tue–Sun 9am–5pm | **Tip** Take in the changing of the guard at the memorial – an impressive spectacle that takes about 40 minutes. It takes place on the first Friday of each month at 10am, except for the months June, August and October, when it takes place on the first Sunday of the month.

99 The Summit of Babilônia
Where wild flowers blossom

The starting point is at the upper end of the Babilônia *favela*, now known throughout Brazil, as the poor, rich, beautiful, and ruthless found themselves here every day in the eponymous telenovela in 2015 (see ch. 6).

A stair-like path leads through the densely vegetated part of the *morro*, or neighborhood. The hill was completely re-planted as part of a reforestation project – over 200,000 trees were introduced, and now the gardens of Babilônia blossom once again over 60 hectares. The walk up to the top is an experience in itself. You may occasionally discover wild toucans, but more often you'll see little monkeys, and even stumble upon historic monuments.

These are ruins from the time when the Portuguese monitored the coast, and also the bunkers that the Brazilian army built here during World War II, camouflaged by the unhindered natural growth. Nowadays, the modest structures are in plain sight and can be visited. The whole of the coast could be surveyed from here, and soldiers kept watch for Nazi U-boats from the observation posts (see ch. 98).

The view from up here is simply superlative: Copacabana and the Sugarloaf Mountain, the bay of Botafogo, Santos Dumont Airport (with, by the way, the shortest landing strip in the world), and Cristo Redentor with his arms spread wide.

On the way back down, you will spot colorful birds in the trees, while butterflies spin through the air. Orchids and bromeliads conjure up magical splashes of color in the natural landscape. The breathtaking view was a key factor using Morro da Babilônia as the setting for the Cannes Film Festival Palm d'Or winning classic film, *Orfeu Negro*, or *Black Orpheus*, in 1959, which portrays the myth of Orpheus and Eurydice set in modern-day carnival in Rio de Janeiro. The film is based on the drama *Orfeu do Carnaval* by Vinícius de Moraes, which premiered in 1956.

Address Morro da Babilônia, Leme, Rio de Janeiro, RJ 22010-060 | **Getting there** Bus 190 or 472 to Avenida Atlântica próximo ao 814, or metro to Cardeal Arcoverde, then about 20-minutes' walk along Avenida Atlântica | **Hours** The residents of the Babilônia *comunidade* organize hiking tours to the summit – a climb of around 200 meters. Book tours at www.coopbabilonia.blogspot.de or with English speaking guide Monika Gläsel Silva at moni-bra-tour@outlook.com | **Tip** Bohemian meeting place La Fiorentina (Avenida Atlântica 458a, Copacabana, Rio de Janeiro, RJ 22010-000) serves fine Italian cuisine. Look for the autographs of many of Rio's greatest artists on the walls.

100__ The Temple of Humanity

National anthem during prayers

A building with a classicist column façade really stands out on Rua Benjamin Constant. It is the "Temple of Humanity," founded in 1881 and home of Brazil's "positivist church."

The intellectual current of Positivism goes back to the French philosopher and natural scientist Auguste Comte (1798–1857), who saw the reform of science and thought as prerequisites to the reform of society.

Written under the beams of the temple are the words: "Love as a principle, order as the basis, progress as the goal." The Positivist motto managed to secure a place on the Brazilian flag with Ordem e Progresso (Order and Progress); only "love" fell by the wayside. The Positivists were, after all, significantly involved in the founding of the Republic of Brazil in 1889.

After years of unrest, slavery was abolished with the "Golden Law" (*Lei Áurea*) in 1888. During this phase of reconstruction and devel-opment, Positivism seemed forward-looking. While it was dismissed as philosophically naïve and noncritical in Europe – Karl Marx spoke of "shitty Positivism" – Comte's thoughts resonated with the aspi-rational middle class in Brazil, with the paradigms of Order and Progress. The Swiss-French activist and Positivist Benjamin Con-stant (1836–1891) thus became the spiritual father of republican politics. The lecturer at the officers' academy propagated industrial-ization and a strong executive, as well as the influence of the military on the political form of the state, which had continuity in Brazil until 1985, including military dictatorships. But democracy was never the goal anyway. The separation of Church and State was, on the oth-er hand, laid down in Brazil 11 years before it happened in France. Today, there are only a few thousand followers of Positivism left. A ceremony takes place here in the "temple" on Sundays, during which the Brazilian national anthem is played.

Address Igreja Positivista do Brasil, Rua Benjamin Constant 74, Glória, Rio de Janeiro, RJ 20241-150 | **Getting there** Metro to Glória, exit Rua da Glória | **Hours** Temporarily not accessible due to restoration | **Tip** Capacete, an alternative cultural space, offers regular events, including video screenings on Wednesday evenings starting at 7.30pm, including food (Rua Benjamin Constant 131, Rio de Janeiro, RJ 20241-150, www.capacete.org).

101 __ The Tile Exhibition
Of hunting and gathering

"I never had the aspiration to be a collector, but I always had fun compiling things, such as the tiles. Plínio Fróes and I found the first ones in a box that we bought from a junk dealer in the 1990s," says Nelson Torzecki. "In time we picked up more and more of them, from Saturday markets on Rua do Lavradio, until at some point we had mountains of tiles." There were in fact 3,000 tiles in their collection by the time the two of them decided to present the most valuable of them in a permanent exhibition.

Antiques in general are the great passion of the two gentlemen, who also own the legendary Rio Scenarium, the party location with a unique atmosphere – packed with a changing array of antiques.

The exhibition comprises 800 exceptional pieces, which amount to a journey through the history of the city of Rio de Janeiro. Following the design tradition of *azulejos*, or tiles, in Portugal, most of the tiles, which once adorned houses, palaces, and churches, are from Rio, but some are also from other parts of the country. Among them are distinctive finds as well as rather plain tiles from a 1970s' bathroom. A tile with Saint George on it can be found among those with saintly motifs from houses in the poorer outskirts of the city. The oldest pieces come from the Santo Antônio Convent in the center of Rio and were sold by a priest in approximately 1927. In this section, with a display that presents other tiles from the convent, you can also find the largest collection of Dutch tiles from the 17th century outside Europe.

Each tile tells its own story from the life of the city. In all, the exhibition documents Portuguese tile art in the 18th and 19th centuries, and the colonial era to modern architecture and art in Brazil, including many art-nouveau decorations and photographs of work by, among others, Portinari Ceramics and landscape architect Roberto Burle Marx.

Address Exposição Azul Cobalto, Galeria Scenarium, Rua do Lavradio 15, Centro, Rio de Janeiro, RJ 20230-070, +55 (21) 3147-9014, www.galeriascenarium.com.br |
Getting there Metro to Carioca | **Hours** Tue–Sat 1–7pm | **Tip** Directly opposite is Rio Scenarium, *the* place to party (Rua do Lavradio 20, Centro, Rio de Janeiro, RJ 20230-070, www.rioscenarium.com.br).

102 __ Tino's Terrace

Spare ribs from the Hill of the Pleased

Severino Santana, who is known as Seu Tino, came to Rio de Janeiro from Pará, in the northern part of Brazil, over 45 years ago, aged just 18. He found work as a builder until he opened a small kiosk in the *favela*, where he sold candy and drinks.

All of his children grew up in Morro dos Prazeres, literally "Hill of Pleasures," in the *favela* above the artistic neighborhood of Santa Teresa. His son Leandro worked in a shoe shop, but in 2002 he lost his job. As an alternative to looking for another job, he set about converting the terrace above his father's kiosk into an informal restaurant. The family was well known and well liked in the *comunidade*, and so the new bar became a popular meeting place overnight. After the pacification of the *favela* in 2011, word of this venue rapidly spread and became a popular insider tip throughout the city for a number of reasons.

For one, the grilled dishes, chicken, and spare ribs *no bafo*, are a dream. They are marinated for a whole day before they are put on the grill, where they cook in smoke under a closed lid. The spice mix is, of course, secret. They are served crispy on the outside, tender and fragrant on the inside with rice, beans, *farofa* (cassava flour), sauce, and fried cassava, the classic side dish from the northeast of Brazil. The ambience is also more reminiscent of the small town in Bahía, where Leandro's mother was born. Secondly, the warmth of the family, who all now work here, is exceptional. Mom Helenice, Bruno, and Adriano serve; Aunty Josefa helps in the kitchen; Tino rules the grill and still looks after his kiosk.

And the third resounding argument for a visit is the breathtaking view of Guanabara Bay with the Sugarloaf at the end of it, the *Christo Redentor* atop Corcovado Mountain, and the Rio-Niterói Bridge – it all compensates for the adventurous ascent through the narrow alleyways of the *favela*.

Address Rua Almirante Alexandrino 3780, Santa Tereza, Rio de Janeiro, RJ 20241-260 | **Getting there** Bus 6 or 7 (from Avenida Gomes Freire 814, corner of Rua Riachuelo, see ch. 49), or taxi to Condomínio Bairro Equitativa, from there take a right and walk up the tarmac road to Campão da Colina | **Hours** Sat, Sun, & holidays 1–9pm; there are only 16 seats so reservation is absolutely necessary, +55 (21) 2225-5780 or +55 (21) 97461-6423; a friend of the family will pick up guests from Condomínio Bairro Equitativa, WhatsApp +55 (21) 99211-5862 | **Tip** There is a lot of graffiti to see in Morro dos Prazeres. Tours in English can be booked with Rio Art Tours (www.rioarttours.org, info@rioarttours.org).

103 The Universal Church

A cathedral like six football pitches

At around 10 o'clock on Sunday mornings, thousands of people stream out of the metro station towards the Universal Church Cathedral. And it really does live up to its name, covering a floor area of 45,000 square meters, the size of about six football pitches.

Mass is given four times on Sunday for 12,000 worshippers. Although the Universal Church has communities all over the city, many prefer to travel here in order to attend mass. "It works better here!" Lucia is certain. "Since I started coming here, my mother has been better." Every Sunday she returns home with two bottles of water blessed by the pastor.

Among the Pentecostal churches, the Universal Church has the biggest following in Brazil. The cathedral was completed in 1999: the twelve-story nave, the eight-story administration building, and four auxiliary buildings, each with four stories and a helicopter landing site. There are facilities for childcare, a cybercafé, fast-food stalls – everything is organized down to the last detail.

Visitors are shown to their seats by uniformed employees, and stairs spiral ever upwards to other entrances. If you come late, you will be seated upstairs. Along with praying and singing, the "Wonder of the Week" presentation on huge screens, including a live appearance of those concerned, is the highlight. The pastor drives out evil by laying his hands on his followers. This is not for the faint hearted – it's not dissimilar to the exorcisms common in American horror films. Conversely, money pours in. Members pay their 10 percent to the church and are very willing to donate. After all, the gospel says that those who pray enough will be rich and healthy. The Universal Church has grown into a multinational company, with 76 radio and 20 TV stations, and influence in high political circles. Crivella, gospel singer, pastor, and nephew of the founder of the Universal Church, has been the mayor of Rio de Janeiro since 2016.

Address Igreja Universal do Reino de Deus Catedral Universal da Fé, Avenida Dom Hélder Câmara (formerly Avenida Suburbana) 4242, Del Castilho, Rio de Janeiro, RJ 20771-003, www.universal.org | **Getting there** Metro to Del Castilho | **Hours** Mass on Sundays, otherwise viewing possible | **Tip** The Nova América shopping mall, just opposite on the other side of the metro exit, is good for browsing (Avenida Pastor Martin Luther King Junior 126, Irajá, Rio de Janeiro, RJ 20765-00, www.novaamerica.com.br).

104_ Valongo Pier
Fatal excavations

The place lay buried under tons of earth for around 150 years. In 2011, laborers began to break up streets and remove cables, pipes, and canals as part of the large-scale project *Porto Maravilha* (Wonderful Harbor) in the run-up to the 2016 Olympic Games. They brought some incredible things to light: archeological finds verified that around 500,000 slaves came ashore here at the harbor between 1769 and 1830.

The demand for free labor had risen drastically due to the enormous gold finds in Minas Gerais. Later, the trading center lost importance, as the trafficking of human beings came under heavy international criticism. In the end, Brazil was the last country in America to officially abolish slavery in 1888.

In 1843, the Valongo Pier, aka Slave Pier, had to make way for the Cais da Imperatriz, or Empress Pier, which was constructed for Teresa Maria Cristina of the Two Sicilies, future wife of the Brazilian Emperor Dom Pedro II.

Archeologists uncovered a very well-preserved harbor facility, as well as a part of Cais da Imperatriz. The differences between the two piers, which were constructed one on top of the other, can be clearly seen: the uneven stones of the old slave pier stand out from the much more precisely cut paving of the structure that was built later. "The Princess of Bourbon stepped on top of the slaves," as some guides on historical tours will tell you.

Later, with the creation of the Republic, the area was redesigned, and these historical artifacts were buried once again. The Cais do Valongo is set to become a United Nations World Heritage Site. The excavations continue to uncover some unique finds, including personal belongings from slaves: bracelets, blue semi-precious stones, which were supposed to protect the wearer from harm, and skillfully carved pipes, which all attest to the dramatic, human history.

Address Cais do Valongo, Avenida Barão de Tefé 91, Saúde, Rio de Janeiro, RJ 20220-460 | **Getting there** Metro to Presidente Vargas or Uruguaiana, then via Avenida Rio Branco to Praça Mauá and on into Avenida Venezuela and Rua Coelho e Castro | **Tip** Lisa Schnittger's tour (in English) tells the story of the Afro-Brazilians, slavery, cultural resistance, and the invention of carnival, and can be booked at info@lisariotours.com.

105_ Vidigal Ecological Park
Auto tire amphitheater

The hundreds of tires are from cars that changed hands in a fashion that was less than 100 percent legal. Apparently, the boss of a tire recycling company rolled them down the hill, and they landed in the *lixão*, the garbage dump, of the Vidigal *favela*. But then three locals made it their mission to tidy up the dumping grounds, which kept them busy for a whole eight years and ended in the creation of an 85,000-square-meter (915,000-square-feet) ecological park.

Not even the neighbors themselves know much about it. If you ask your conductor, "Where do I have to get off for the ecological park?" he'll usually have no idea what you're talking about. So it's better to ask for Estação Biroscão and then turn off from the street and onto a path, and then climb down on the aforementioned tires into this small botanical paradise. The place will simply astonish you. You would more likely expect to find the peace sign, cut neat and tidy out of prickly tropical plants, in the front garden of a middle-class neighborhood. And there are not many from the *comunidade* itself who have a special connection to this kind of designed nature.

In Vidigal, with its 30,000 residents, the urban life of the asphalt is predominant. "Other *favelas* are often more in touch with nature, with people cultivating plants from their homelands," says Emel, who takes tours through Vidigal and likes to visit the nature park.

It is quite remarkable what the three initiators have made out of the former garbage dump. Alongside the well-kept gardens, there is now a small amphitheater, also made out of car tires, where music events are being planned. At the top of the park, you will be rewarded with a fantastic view of the bay and the beaches of Leblon and Ipanema. The initiators have further projects in mind for the former garbage dump, which now receives support from Princeton University.

Address Vidigal, Estação Biroscão, Rio de Janeiro, RJ 22450-270 | **Getting there** Metro L1, L4 to Jardim de Alha, then mototaxi, or walk to Praça dos Direitos Humanos, or take any bus along Avenida Niemeyer to Praça dos Direitos Humanos, then mini bus or mototaxi – ask the driver to stop at Biroscão | **Tip** There is also a walking trail up Morro Dois Irmãos, from which you will find the best views of the heart-shaped lake, Lagoa Rodrigo de Freitas. Rio Art Tours organizes hiking tours to Vidigal. Contact emel.mangel@gmail.com for information and booking.

106__ Vila do Largo
Home office

If you look through the wrought-iron gate from the outside, your first impression may be that these are private apartments. In a certain way that's true, because these are apartments, but at the same time artists' studios, which have been set up inside these historic houses after a comprehensive renovation.

The ensemble of houses is originally from the 1930s, when a classic general store was to be found in the main house. At some point, the shop owner started to rent out the rooms above the shop, first to traveling salesmen, and later to permanent tenants too. Thus the whole complex ultimately became residential.

The architect Carlos Rangel bought a total of 80 percent of the "villas," had the apartments renovated to a high standard – all of them have been left faithfully in brick construction – and maintained its architecture completely. The result is a kind of community of 26 studios and workshops; the same families are still living in the other eight apartments as before the restoration. The artists live here on site. The architect Rangel called these studios *casas de ofício* (home offices). In house 19, for example, is the company Prime Design, which designs quirky furniture and accessories. Or there is the sculptor Pat Newman in house 13, who has a three-story studio because the original floor plan of the buildings with small apartments was maintained. He hauls the plaster for his work up to the third story with a homemade elevator.

Every day is Open Studio Day at all of the studios – you can visit them any time. There are also lots of events, from the disco in the studios to film days and various gastronomical events. There's fantastic coffee at Café Secreto in house 8 every day, prepared by Renato, who runs the charming coffeehouse with Gabriela. And to go with it, chocolate or orange cake, all homemade and just as delicious as the fresh bread.

Address Vila do Largo, Rua Gago Coutinho 4–8, Rio de Janeiro, RJ 22221-070 | **Getting there** Metro to Largo do Machado | **Tip** The Imperial Hotel offers good value in a prime location (Rua do Catete 186, Catete, Rio de Janeiro, RJ 22220-000, www.imperialhotel.com.br).

107 __ Vila Silveira
Eccentric for billionaires

The most beautiful, intact, art-nouveau building in Rio de Janeiro was built in 1915 by the eccentric Italian architect Antonio Virzi. Today, the magnificent, three-story building belongs to Eike Batista. He was, for a short time, the seventh richest person in the world and was praised as Brazil's model businessman. In the years 2012 through 2013, the entrepreneur filled the headlines of the world's business papers, until the multi-billionaire crashed and went bankrupt.

The building cannot be accessed at the moment, but the architecture is just as impressive from the outside. The asymmetrical columns are decorated with fine stucco, the doors and windows with filigree forgings. The entrance door is adorned with a golden door handle in an elegant snake form.

The asymmetric structure of the outer façade creates a strong ensemble and will also excite art historians. The work of the architect Virzi is often compared with that of the famous Catalan architect Antonio Gaudí.

The eccentric building was originally built for Gervásio Renault da Silveira, the producer of the famous Nogueira Elixir, a tonic that was, at the time, deemed to have miraculous properties. Virzi also designed Silveira's famous factory building. The building, as ever with Virzi, followed an unconventional design: the first two stories were cylindrical, and the upper stories quadratic. In 1970 this almost surreal industrial memorial was unceremoniously demolished amidst protests from the population. "Nothing about Virzi is predictable, symmetric, or rectangular," architectural experts decree, "if he had worked in Europe, he would have been world famous."

There are also other buildings by Virzi in Rio, including Rio Casa Sem Vidros (Rio Windowless House) at Rua Sá Ferreira 80 and the American Cinema on Avenida Atlântica to admire – as well as around 1,000 art-deco buildings throughout the city.

Address Rua do Rússel 734, Rio de Janeiro, RJ 22210-010 | **Getting there** Metro to Gloria | **Tip** The house at 710 Rua Rússel is another architectural jewel to be admired. Edifício Milton, one of the most elegant addresses in the city with an impressive green marble portal by Adolpho Dourado Lopes, was built in 1929.

108_ Villarino Bar

Of barmen and artists

In 1943, a Spanish man came ashore in the harbor of Rio de Janeiro after an adventurous passage. Like many others, he had hopes of a better life. After several jobs as a barman, he found his place in Bar Villarino. Fine food and local and imported liquors were on offer, quite an attraction at the time. In 1958, after his training, Antônio Vásquez became a partner. Business was booming, as the location in the middle of downtown rapidly gave the bar an endless supply of revelers. They ranged from employees from the business and legal sectors to bohemians, artists, and laborers – in other words, anyone who was glad for good conversation in the late afternoon over a couple of drinks and a tasty snack.

Antônio got to know many celebrities personally, and photo boards in the bar serve as a reminder, when Rio was still the capital. Artists such as Emilio di Cavalcanti, pioneer of modern art, or Augusto Rodrigues, artist, cartoonist, illustrator, and poet. Or the bossa-nova musician Ary Barroso, who was inspired to write the words for the world-famous song "Aquarela do Brasil" here in this very bar. In 1956, Antônio met Vinícius de Moraes – lyricist of the song "Girl from Ipanema" – at Villarino. He was a regular for years and always enjoyed a good whiskey.

In 2013, many cultural celebrities were invited to celebrate Bar Villarino's 60th birthday. Caricaturist Chico Caruso with his twin brother Paulo, icon of modern satire in Brazil, raved about how ideas used to fly around this room. The furnishings are unchanged to this day, and the bar still gives off a bit of the charm of the past, even though it has become quieter here in comparison to the neighboring bars.

What has always stayed the same is the excellent service of the bar staff – that must have always been close to Antônio's heart after his own years in training – and the outstanding quality of the food.

Address Bar Villarino, Avenida Calógeras 6, on the corner of Avenida Presidente Wilson, Rio de Janeiro, RJ 20030-070, +55 (21) 2240-1627, www.villarino.com.br, csvillarino@gmail.com | **Getting there** Metro to Cinelândia, then via Avenida Rio Branco and Rua Santa Luzia to Avenida Calógeras | **Hours** Mon–Fri noon–9pm | **Tip** Just next door, at the popular Os Bar, they serve delicious *cachaças* and little snacks as an aperitif (Avenida Calógeras 18 A, Centro, Rio de Janeiro, RJ 20030-070).

109__ Vó Alzira's Cake Factory

Deliciously homemade!

Coconut, banana, or orange flavored, or chocolate topped with sprinkles for a child's birthday – these are the cakes you won't find in just any bakery. They are the kinds of treats traditionally baked only by grannies or moms for their beloved families – or here at the Fábrica de Bolo Vó Alzira, or Granny Alzira's Cake Factory. And that's one thing that makes this place so popular, as very few people in Rio still have the time to make their own cakes from scratch.

Homemade cakes are enjoyed all over Brazil. People often eat a slice for breakfast and at birthday parties, where the four-tier cake is taller than the birthday girl or boy. In Rio, the one-tier variety is popular and essential for any kind of party.

The cake recipes of Vó, or Granny, Alzira caused quite a stir when she first began baking. She was working in the bar of a friend, who asked her to bake cakes for his customers.

Within a short time, she was inundated with orders, and so her whole family joined the business, with husband Claudio mixing the batter. For two years, they ran the business out of their home, and then from their popcorn shop, until finally popcorn made way for cake production.

Seven years later, Fábrica de Bolo Vó Alzira has over 10 branches in Rio alone and makes what many consider the best cake in the city. Up to 110,000 cakes a month are baked daily in 20 different flavors, filled or glazed. In the meantime the cake factory functions as a franchise system through the whole state of Rio de Janeiro, but the recipe remains a secret to this day. Every branch has to buy and use the original cake mixture from Granny Alzira.

But the family is not finished. An expansion into the northeast of the country, perhaps also to Argentina, is planned. If there's no birthday party coming up, just visit a shop for a delicious slice, fresh and warm out of the oven if you're lucky.

Address Fábrica de Bolo, Rua da Relação 39, Loja C, Centro, Rio de Janeiro, RJ 22231-010, www.fabricadebolo.com | **Getting there** Metro to Carioca or Cinelândia | **Tip** Nearby, the modernist Catedral Metropolitana, built in 1976, just behind the ultra modern Petrobras building, is worth seeing (Avenida Chile 245, Centro, Rio de Janeiro, RJ 20031-170, www.catedral.com.br).

110_ Wagner's Bar

Fresh fish from a football legend

It takes no more than 15 minutes to get to the other side of Guanabara Bay to Niterói on the ferry. You can drive across the 13-kilometer-long Rio-Niterói Bridge, an impressive example of the work of architect Oscar Niemeyer.

In addition to the classic sights, such as Niemeyer Way and the Museu de Arte Contemporânea (MAC), or the Museum of Contemporary Art, the São Pedro Fish Market is an experience. Every day, everyone from housewives to the chefs of the city's top restaurants, including the best sushi restaurant in Rio, buy fresh fish at the biggest fish market in the state of Rio de Janeiro. A total of almost 40 stalls offer tuna, cod, sardines, salmon, and shellfish, as well as more rare seafood, such as gigantic groupers. Walking around the historic market is a feast for the eyes – and the nostrils. Italian immigrants, who had fled from the poverty in their home country after World War II, established this fish market together in 1951.

On the first floor, 10 or so restaurants group their tables around two huge aquariums filled with live fish. If you like, you can ask the server to roast, fry, or grill the very fresh fish you have just purchased. Or you can simply order fried bream in Bar do Wagner, which has a legendary reputation. The shellfish and the fish soup, or *caldeirada*, are also delicious.

The bar is well known and well loved, largely because Sebastião Wágner de Souza e Silva, the ex-goalkeeper for the Botafogo Soccer Club, Brazilian national champions, serves the ice-cold beer and fried fish here personally. After his career as a footballer he worked as a taxi driver and a kiosk owner, but now he's convinced he's found his place. His sociable manner when he talks shop with the guests, and the top quality of the fish dishes have made the restaurant a popular meeting place. And after dinner on the weekend, the beers tend to flow…

Address O Mercado de Peixes São Pedro, Box 209, Rua Visconde do Rio Branco 55, Ponta D'Areia, Niterói, RJ 24020-000 | **Getting there** Ferry from Praça XV (15 minutes) to Niterói, Praça Araribóia, then straight on, on the left of the main street, to the market | **Hours** Tue–Sat 6am–6pm, Sun 6am–noon | **Tip** You definitely shouldn't miss other great works of the genius architect, which can be found on Caminho Niemeyer.

111 The Zeppelin Hangar
The home of the Hindenburg

"We ran onto the streets and saw the silver Zeppelin floating above the bay, saw how everyone was looking out of their windows – I will never forget it for the rest of my life," is how 89-year-old Nelsina still remembers it today. The excitement of the Cariocas was boundless when the 236-meter-long airship *Graf Zeppelin* came to Rio for the first time, from Friedrichshafen via Seville and Recife, in May 1930.

Getúlio Vargas, Brazilian president at the time, decided in the course of his policy of equipping Brazil with future-oriented technology, to install an airship landing site in Santa Cruz in order to make regular aviation possible. Everything, right down to the smallest detail, was imported from Germany. The construction of the hall – 270 meters long, 50 meters wide, and 54 meters tall – took three years, and it was inaugurated in 1936. The *Graf Zeppelin* landed here, as did the *Hindenburg*, during the short heyday of Zeppelin aviation that lasted until the *Hindenburg*'s tragic accident on May 6, 1937, in which 36 people were killed.

The Santa Cruz hangar is now an industrial memorial in the middle of a military base and is looked after with great effort. "If something breaks, we actually need a mountain climber to do the repair work," says Jonas, who trains the next generation here on site. On the side of one of the door leaves – each weighs 80 tons – which can be moved using the strength of 30 people if the motor happens to fail, is a sign with the inscription *Gutehoffnungshütte Oberhausen – Allemanha* with two "l"s instead of just one, but that too is preserved in it's original state.

Today, fighter planes are serviced here – they look like ants in the only surviving Zeppelin hangar in the world. Thirty million liters of Zeppelin propellant were once stored in the blue globe next to it, providing the fuel the Zeppelin needed to rise up into the air.

PRINCE HENRY'S HIGH SCHOOL LEARNING RESOURCE CENTRE

Address Hangar do Zeppelin, Força Aérea Brasileira, Rua do Império, Santa Cruz, Rio de Janeiro, RJ 23555-02 | **Getting there** Train from Central to Santa Cruz (around 1 hour), then minibus from Canto do Rio near the station to the Santa Cruz military base | **Hours** The hangar is on a military base, so visits must be announced and written permission gained for foreigners in advance by writing to scsbasc@hotmail.com. This process can take up to three weeks, but the date of your visit can then be arranged flexibly; inquiries at Comunicação Social +55 (21) 3078-0362 or +55 (21) 3078-0389, Sergente Aruda or Felipe Pinha | **Tip** The old Fazenda Real building, now Batalhão Vilagran Cabrita, in the Praça Ruão near to Santa Cruz metro station is worth seeing.

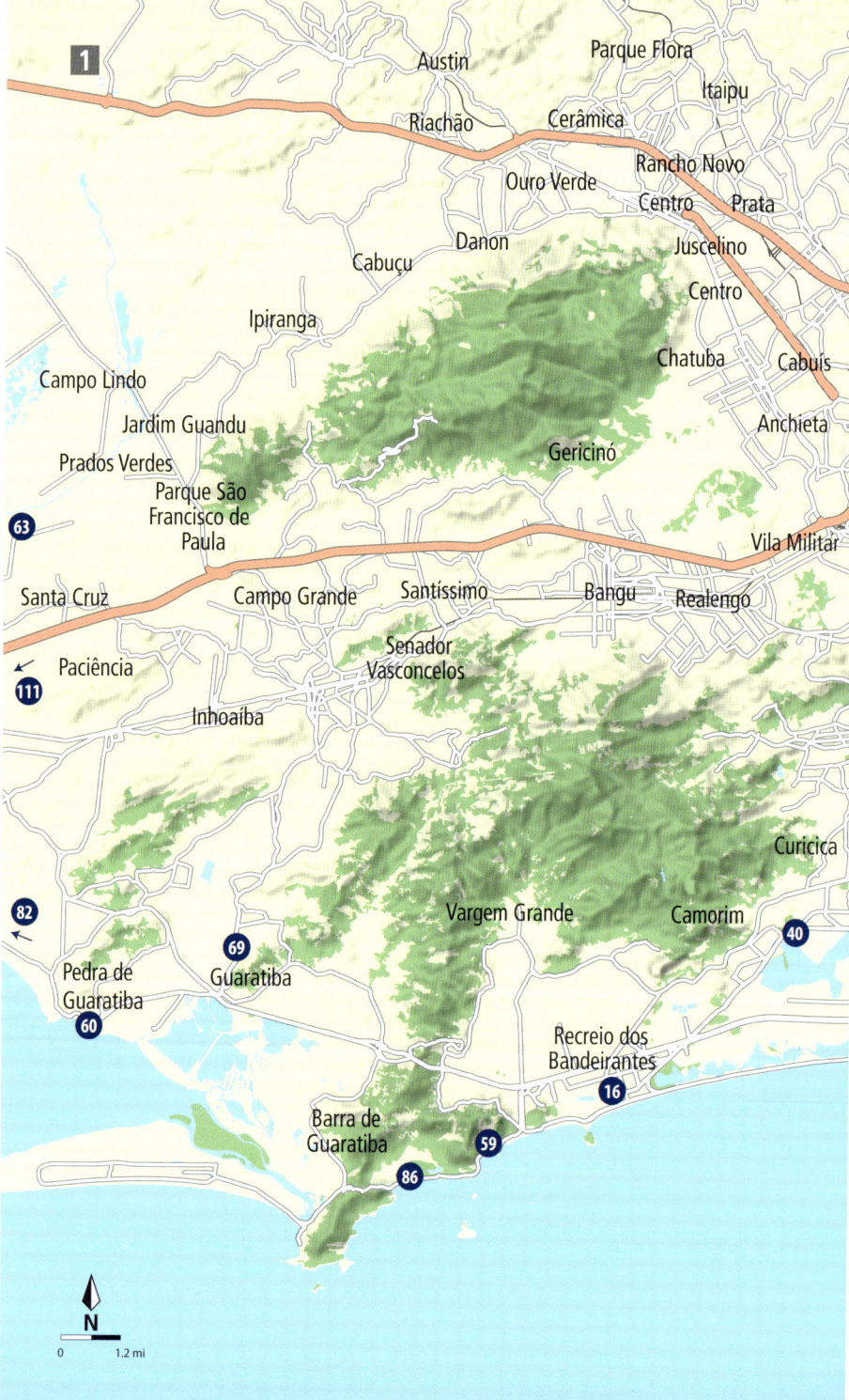

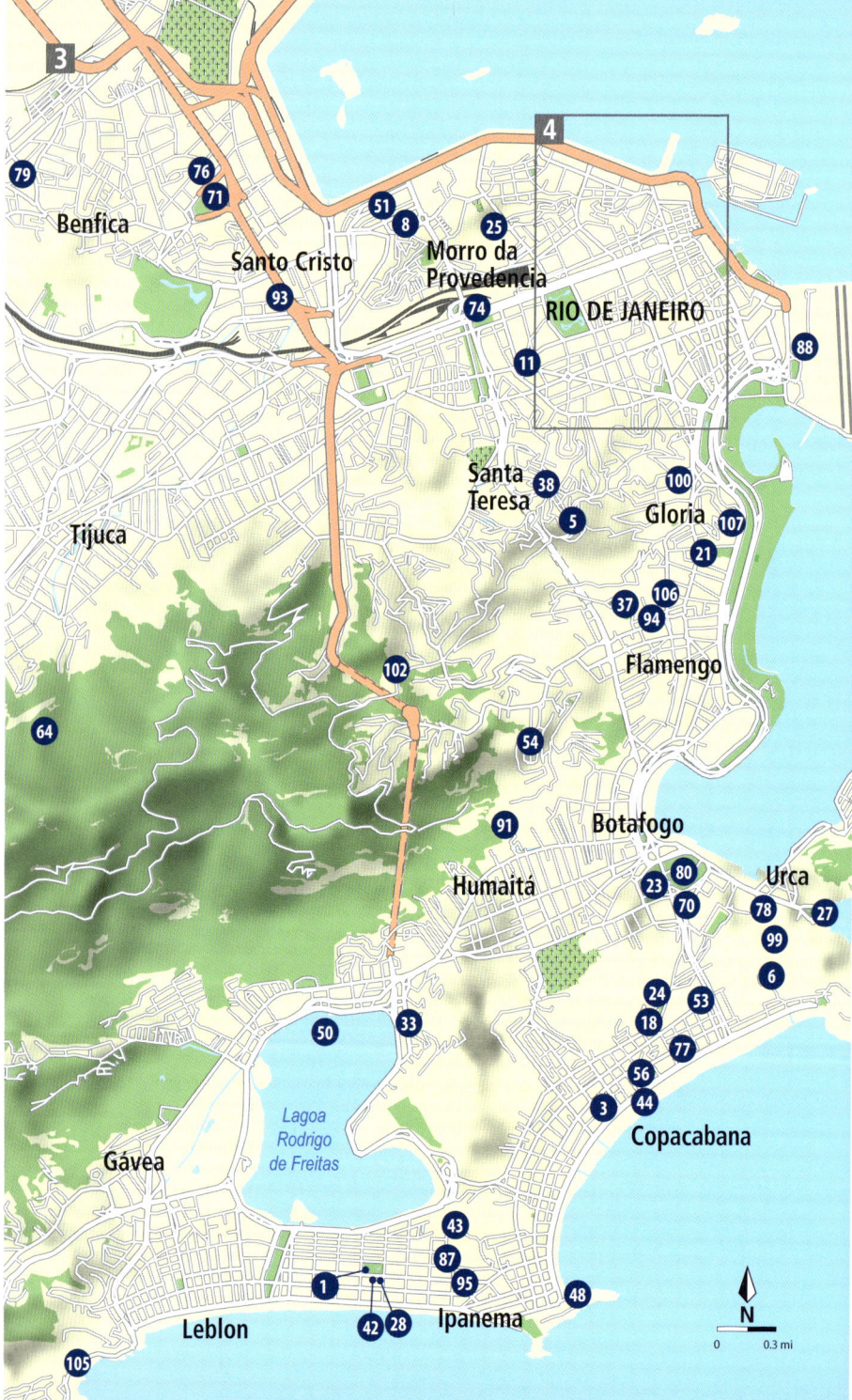

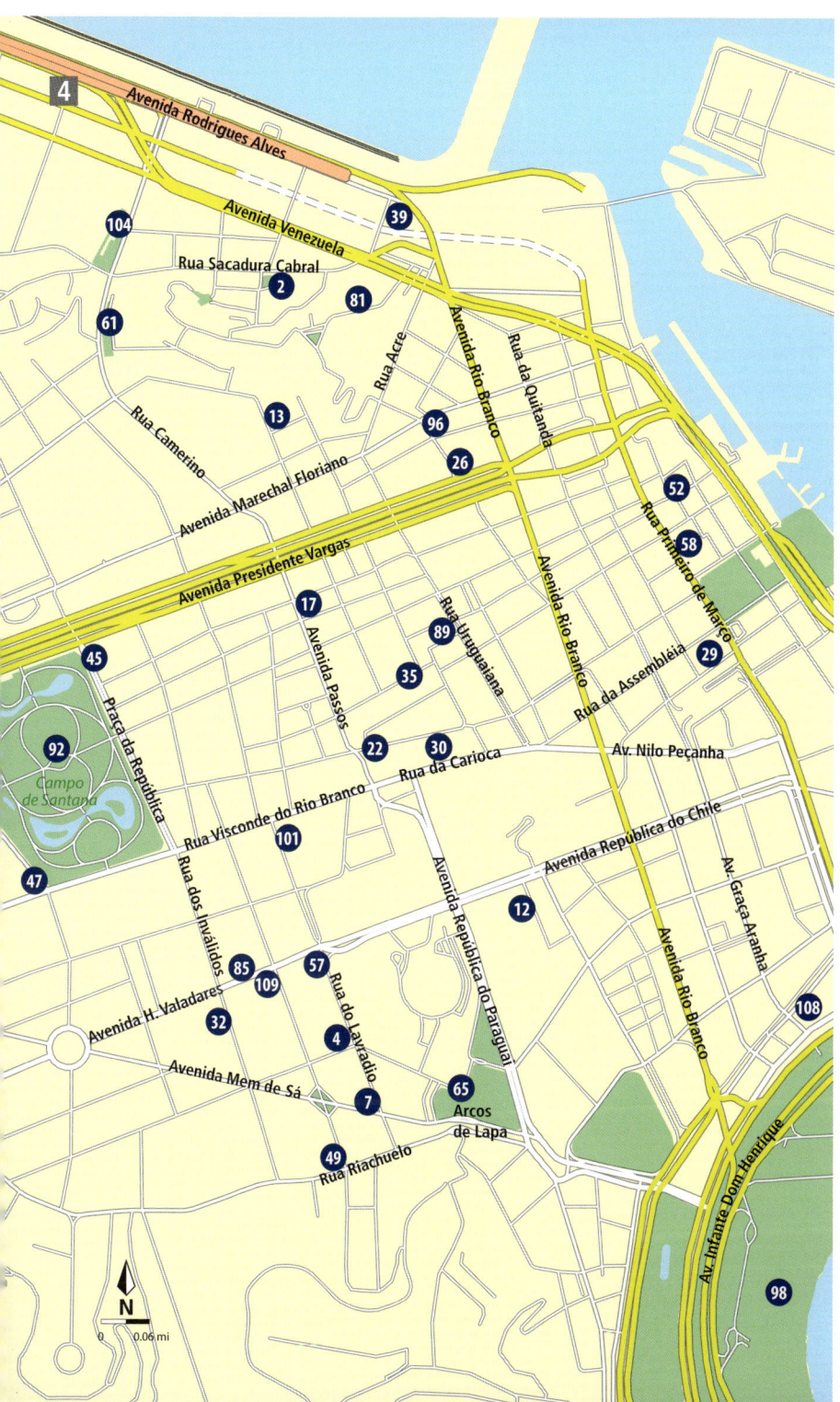

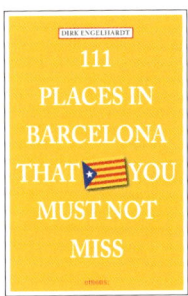

Dirk Engelhardt
111 PLACES IN BARCELONA
THAT YOU MUST NOT MISS
ISBN 978-3-95451-353-6

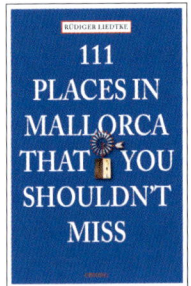

Rüdiger Liedtke
111 PLACES ON MALLORCA
THAT YOU SHOULDN'T MISS
ISBN 978-3-95451-281-2

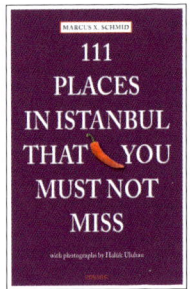

Marcus X. Schmid
111 PLACES IN ISTANBUL
THAT YOU MUST NOT MISS
ISBN 978-3-95451-423-6

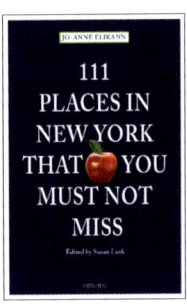

Jo-Anne Elikann
111 PLACES IN NEW YORK
THAT YOU MUST NOT MISS
ISBN 978-3-95451-052-8

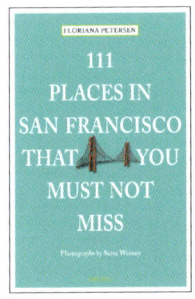

Floriana Petersen, Steve Werney
111 PLACES IN SAN
FRANCISCO THAT YOU
MUST NOT MISS
ISBN 978-3-95451-609-4

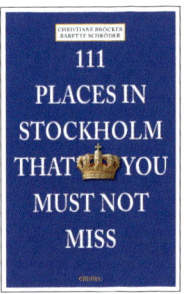

Christiane Bröcker,
Babette Schröder
111 PLACES IN STOCKHOLM
THAT YOU MUST NOT MISS
ISBN 978-3-95451-459-5

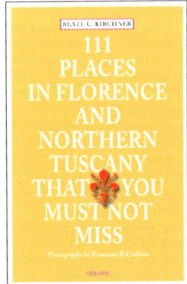

Beate C. Kirchner
111 PLACES IN FLORENCE
AND NORTHERN TUSCANY
THAT YOU MUST NOT MISS
ISBN 978-3-95451-613-1

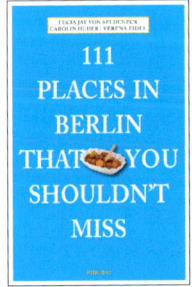

Lucia Jay von Seldeneck,
Carolin Huder, Verena Eidel
111 PLACES IN BERLIN
THAT YOU SHOULDN'T MISS
ISBN 978-3-95451-208-9

Laurel Moglen, Julia Posey
111 PLACES IN LOS ANGELES
THAT YOU SHOULDN'T MISS
ISBN 978-3-95451-884-5

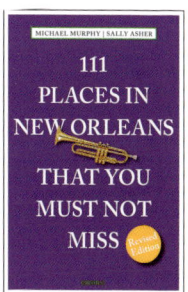

Michael Murphy, Sall Asher
111 PLACES IN NEW ORLEANS THAT YOU MUST NOT MISS
ISBN 978-3-95451-645-2

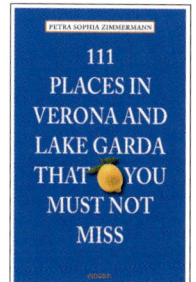

Petra Sophia Zimmermann
111 PLACES IN VERONA AND LAKE GARDA THAT YOU MUST NOT MISS
ISBN 978-3-95451-611-7

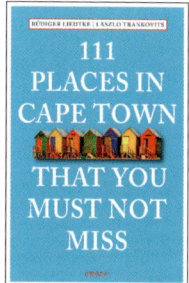

Rüdiger Liedtke,
Laszlo Trankovits
111 PLACES IN CAPE TOWN THAT YOU MUST NOT MISS
ISBN 978-3-95451-610-0

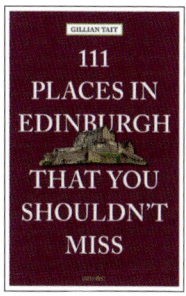

Gillian Tait
111 PLACES IN EDINBURGH THAT YOU SHOULDN'T MISS
ISBN 978-3-95451-883-8

Rike Wolf
111 PLACES IN HAMBURG THAT YOU SHOULDN'T MISS
ISBN 978-3-95451-234-8

Giulia Castelli Gattinara,
Mario Verin
111 PLACES IN MILAN THAT YOU MUST NOT MISS
ISBN 978-3-95451-331-4

John Sykes
111 PLACES IN LONDON THAT YOU SHOULDN'T MISS
ISBN 978-3-95451-346-8

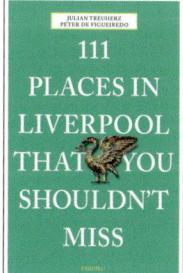

Julian Treuherz,
Peter de Figueiredo
111 PLACES IN LIVERPOOL THAT YOU SHOULDN'T MISS
ISBN 978-3-95451-769-5

Rüdiger Liedtke
111 PLACES IN MUNICH THAT YOU SHOULDN'T MISS
ISBN 978-3-95451-222-5

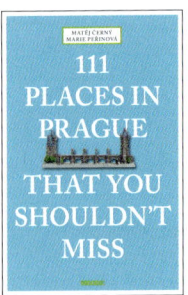

Matěj Černý, Marie Peřinová
**111 PLACES IN PRAGUE
THAT YOU SHOULDN'T MISS**
ISBN 978-3-7408-0144-1

Sybil Canac, Renée Grimaud,
Katia Thomas
**111 PLACES IN PARIS THAT
YOU SHOULDN'T MISS**
ISBN 978-3-7408-0159-5

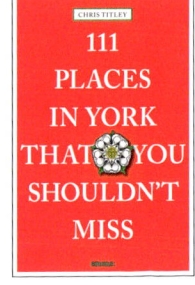

Chris Titley
**111 PLACES IN YORK THAT
YOU SHOULDN'T MISS**
ISBN 978-3-95451-768-8

Kathrin Bielfeldt,
Raymond Wong, Jürgen Bürger
**111 PLACES IN HONG KONG
THAT YOU SHOULDN'T MISS**
ISBN 978-3-95451-936-1

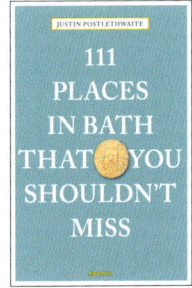

Justin Postlethwaite
**111 PLACES IN BATH THAT
YOU SHOULDN'T MISS**
ISBN 978-3-7408-0146-5

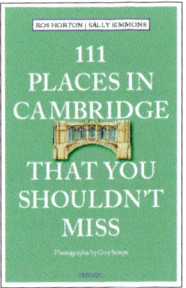

Rosalind Horton,
Sally Simmons, Guy Snape
**111 PLACES IN CAMBRIDGE
THAT YOU SHOULDN'T MISS**
ISBN 978-3-7408-0147-2

Frank McNally
**111 PLACES IN DUBLIN
THAT YOU SHOULDN'T MISS**
ISBN 978-3-95451-649-0

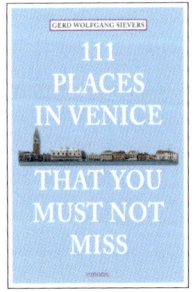

Gerd Wolfgang Sievers
**111 PLACES IN VENICE
THAT YOU MUST NOT MISS**
ISBN 978-3-95451-460-1

Sharon Fernandes
**111 PLACES IN NEW DELHI
THAT YOU MUST NOT MISS**
ISBN 978-3-95451-648-3

Many thanks to:

Augusto Barros, Capela Magdalena, Maria do Rozario Barros, Luciano Caetano Ferreira, Renato Campos, São Cristóvão de Futebol e Regatas, Paulo Dallier, Ana Christina Fiedler, RioTour, Ana Fonseca, Bia Novellino and Bia Sartorio, Role Carioca, Francisco and Milton, Fabrica Biscoito Globo, Gabriel and Renato, Biblioteca Social Fábio Luz, Moniva Glasel Silva, Regina Hettenhausen van Carvajho, Christoph Hoefer, Ivo Korytowski, literaturaeriodejaneiro. blogspot.com, Emel Mangel, RioArttour, Isnard Manso, Nelsina Mendes, Carmen and Gerhard Strunz, München, Alexandre Macieira, Hudson Rafael Moreira dos Santos, Sciencas Aeronauticas, Marcia and Filipe Pinha, Força Aérea Brasileira, Jorge Mourão, Archivos Impossibles, Fernanda Motta, Jonas do Nascimento Alves, Tay Nacimento, Silvia Nunes, Ludmila Pereira, Irene Cristina Portela, Vinicius Roberto Barbosa Leal, Antonia Aila Aiencar de Aliveira, Caio Cezar de Carvalho Pontes and Omar, MAST, Ana Rabello, Instituto Casa do Choro, Andrea Rüthlein and Matthias Lukoschek, Lisa Schnittger, Denise Terra, Ozzi Terra Vasconcellos, Vanessa Maria Vlan de Castro, Renate Wolf.

A note in your own interest

A guide from the community is always recommended for the places in this guidebook that will take you into a *favela*. Each *favela* is a kind of community (*comunidade*), where the houses are built close to each other, the windows are usually open, and often people do not withdraw into their own private spheres. When you take a walk through a *comunidade*, it is possible to encroach too closely on residents or to stumble ignorantly into an unsafe situation. Likewise, not everyone wants to be photographed. It is not possible for outsiders to judge where conflict may arise. So please hire an experienced guide who lives in the *favela* to avoid situations you are not equipped to deal with and rather enjoy your experience. The community also benefits from the income generated by tours.

The author

Beate C. Kirchner was born in 1960 in Munich and studied in Florence and Munich. After attaining her degree in political science, she worked for many years as a managing editor for German magazines. Today she is an independent journalist and author in the fields of business, politics, and travel. She visits Florence and Tuscany several times a year.

The photographer

Jorge Vasconcellos, a native Carioca, studied at the Associação Brasileira de Artes Fotográfica (Brazilian Association of Photographic Arts), Estácio de Sá University and Cândido Mendes University. He organizes photography courses and tours in Rio de Janeiro and is co-owner of the photography agency ICON Foto Brasil. Expositions at FotoRio in 2004, 2005, 2007, 2009 and 2011, at Biennale of Fotografie of the City of Rio de Janeiro and at the Festival of Fotografie of Juiz de Fora, MG.